Integrating SEL into Your Curriculum

In this helpful new book, John Dacey, Gian Criscitiello, and Maureen Devlin show you how to seamlessly infuse social and emotional learning into your curriculum. With the growing emphasis on student assessment and learning outcomes, many teachers find they lack the time and the encouragement to begin implementing SEL techniques into their instruction. This book offers a solution in the form of practical lesson plans for grades 3–5 in ELA, math, social studies, and science—all of which can be implemented without tedious preparation and all of which are designed to boost creativity, cooperation, concentration, and critical thinking. Your students will learn how to . . .

- Evaluate the costs and benefits of their decision-making;
- Connect daily choices to an overarching sense of purpose;
- Judge independently and pursue self-awareness;
- Assess, harness, and transform emotions as a strategic resource;
- Gain energy from personal values and commitments; and
- Practice mindfulness and think positively.

Each chapter contains a number of reproducible tools that can be photocopied from the book or downloaded as eResources from the book product page at www.routledge.com/9781138632066.

John Dacey is Professor Emeritus of the Lynch School of Education at Boston College in Chestnut Hill.

Gian Criscitiello teaches mathematics to students with language-based learning differences at the Carroll School in Lincoln, MA.

Maureen Devlin is a National Board Certified Teacher (NBCT) and a practicing elementary school educator in Wayland, Massachusetts.

Also Available from Routledge Eye On Education
(www.routledge.com/eyeoneducation)

Passionate Learners, 2nd Edition:
How to Engage and Empower Your Students
Pernille Ripp

Passionate Readers:
The Art of Reaching and Engaging Every Child
Pernille Ripp

Learning on Your Feet:
Incorporating Physical Activity into the
K–8 Classroom
Brad Johnson and Melody Jones

Motivating Struggling Learners:
10 Ways to Build Student Success
Barbara R. Blackburn

History Class Revisited:
Tools and Projects to Engage Middle School Students
in Social Studies
Jody Passanisi

The Flexible ELA Classroom:
Practical Tools for Differentiated Instruction in Grades 4–8
Amber Chandler

The Flexible SEL Classroom:
Practical Ways to Build Social-Emotional Learning in Grades 4–8
Amber Chandler

Integrating SEL into Your Curriculum

Practical Lesson Plans for Grades 3–5

John Dacey, Ph.D.
Gian Criscitiello, M.A.
Maureen Devlin, M.A.

Routledge
Taylor & Francis Group
NEW YORK AND LONDON

First published 2018
by Routledge
711 Third Avenue, New York, NY 10017

and by Routledge
2 Park Square, Milton Park, Abingdon, Oxon, OX14 4RN

Routledge is an imprint of the Taylor & Francis Group, an informa business

© 2018 Taylor & Francis

The right of John Dacey, Gian Criscitiello, and Maureen Devlin to be identified as authors of this work has been asserted by them in accordance with sections 77 and 78 of the Copyright, Designs and Patents Act 1988.

All rights reserved. The purchase of this copyright material confers the right on the purchasing institution to photocopy or download pages which bear the eResources icon and a copyright line at the bottom of the page. No other parts of this book may be reprinted or reproduced or utilized in any form or by any electronic, mechanical, or other means, now known or hereafter invented, including photocopying and recording, or in any information storage or retrieval system, without permission in writing from the publishers.

Trademark notice: Product or corporate names may be trademarks or registered trademarks, and are used only for identification and explanation without intent to infringe.

Library of Congress Cataloging-in-Publication Data
A catalog record for this book has been requested

ISBN: 978-1-138-63153-3 (hbk)
ISBN: 978-1-138-63206-6 (pbk)
ISBN: 978-1-315-20847-3 (ebk)

Typeset in Palatino and Myriad Pro
by Apex CoVantage, LLC

Visit the eResources: www.routledge.com/9781138632066

To teacher Sylvia Schotts, who was bravely embedding SEL in her fourth grade curriculum through all the years when that just wasn't done!

Contents

eResources .... *ix*
Meet the Authors .... *xi*
Acknowledgments .... *xiii*

1. Why You Will Want to Integrate SEL into Your Curriculum............ 1

Part I: Self-Awareness

2. Be Authentic... 7

3. Practice Mindfulness.. 25

Part II: Self-Management

4. Think Positively.. 37

5. Be in Control... 55

6. Think Independently 69

7. Be Resilient.. 81

Part III: Social Awareness

8. Cooperate and Compete Successfully 93

9. Neither Be a Bully nor Be Bullied 103

Part IV: Relationship Skills

10. Build Successful Friendships............................... 113

11. Demonstrate Leadership 123

Part V: Responsible Decision-Making

12. Think Creatively 139

13. Think Critically and Wisely 155

Part VI: Achieving Teaching Goals More Effectively

14. Help for Harried Teachers 173

15. Multiple Means of Measuring Your Students' SEL 183

16. The Future of SEL 189

References *197*

eResources

The reproducibles in this book are also available on the Routledge website as free eResources.

They are indicated in the book by the eResources logo. You can access the eResources by visiting the book product page: www.routledge.com/9781138632066. Click on the tab that says "eResources" and select the files. They will begin downloading to your computer.

Meet the Authors

Dr. John Dacey received a B.A. in Social Science from Binghamton University in 1963. He then enrolled at Cornell University, where he received an M.A.T. in social science in 1964 and a Ph.D. in developmental and educational psychology in 1966.

He joined the faculty of Boston College that year and still teaches there as Professor in the Developmental and Educational Psychology Program. John has appeared on The Today Show and on NPR, both several times. He has a small practice as a psychotherapist, licensed in Massachusetts. He is an expert on anxiety in childhood and has a nationally tested COPE program used by parents, teachers, and psychotherapists to relieve the symptoms of this syndrome.

He is the author of 17 books on the subjects of anxiety, creativity, and human development, including *Your Anxious Child*, 2nd Ed., and *Your Child's Social and Emotional Well-Being*. He has received public service awards from Newton, Peabody, and Roxbury, Massachusetts.

He has three adult children: Julie (novelist), Jennifer (Professor of Public Health, Tufts University), and Kristen (photographer). His wife Linda is Professor of Mathematics Education at Lesley University. He has nine wonderful grandchildren ranging in age from 12 to 22.

Gian Criscitiello received his Masters in Education from Wheelock College in Boston in 1993 and has worked with grade 3–6 public school students as a teacher for 13 years and then as a principal for five years. He returned to the classroom in 2009 to teach in an international school in the West Indies for four years and is currently teaching mathematics to students with language-based learning differences at the Carroll School in Lincoln, MA.

Gian is a musician, carpenter, transatlantic sailor, and an outdoors enthusiast and firmly believes students learn best, in the social-emotional realm and academically, when they make connections to the world outside the classroom and are challenged by new situations.

Maureen Devlin is a National Board Certified Teacher (NBCT) and a practicing elementary school educator in Wayland, Massachusetts. Maureen has taught elementary school for 31 years. During that time, she has engaged in a large number of professional learning and outreach activities including teaching teacher candidates at Framingham State University and Northeastern University; presenting at local and national conferences; co-leading #edchat on Twitter; sharing ideas, reflection, and research via her blog, Teach Children Well; and collaborating with educators both locally and nationally via professional learning and leadership activities with the Massachusetts Teachers Association, National Education Association, and the Massachusetts Department of Elementary and Secondary Education Teachers Advisory Cabinet. Maureen has also been an honored guest at The Bill and Melinda Gates Foundation-supported 2016 Elevating and Celebrating Effective Teaching and Teachers (ECET2) Conference in San Diego, and a co-organizer for the Massachusetts ECET2 Teach All Children event in October 2017.

Acknowledgments

The authors would like to acknowledge the help and support of the following people:

The staff at Routledge, including our editor, Lauren Davis, for her guidance and many kindnesses; copyeditor, Christina Tang-Bernas, John DeFalco, sales;

Kevin Kelsey, project manager at Apex CoVantage;

Boston College research assistant, senior Mary Kate O'Neill;

The late Dr. Steven Brion-Meisels, who introduced us and so many others to the concept of SEL, and the tremendous need for it in the schools;

And last but not least, our wonderfully supportive spouses, Dr. Linda Dacey, TK.

1

Why You Will Want to Integrate SEL into Your Curriculum

> The survival of the human race depends at least as much on the cultivation of social and emotional intelligence as it does on the development of technical knowledge and skills.
>
> Dr. Roger Weissberg, CIO, CASEL

In our preparation for this book, we have interviewed dozens of teachers in the US, Britain, and 12 other countries. They agree with Dr. Weissberg on the importance of social and emotional learning (SEL), and say that most curricula are too deeply invested in academic learning (AL: facts and procedures). However, they also concur that universally, most teachers are evaluated by their students' success on multiple-choice governmental tests of AL. Therefore, understandably, the likelihood that the world's teaching corps will spend much time on SEL is low.

This result is injurious to our children and to our societies. SEL is needed, among other reasons, to remediate the surging number and severity of student problem behaviors. Students universally are receiving messages about social and emotional norms through the media, and at a faster rate than we have ever seen before. Many of these messages are problematic—selfish, cynical, and often sexual.[1] Teachers want to help rectify this trend. Most genuinely want to make a contribution to the life success of their pupils, and they don't believe that AL alone does that. Many teachers resent being forced to "teach to the test."

Furthermore, there is significant evidence that neither governmental tests, nor school grades, nor college readiness tests such as the SAT in the US, are good predictors of success in life, or even of college grades,[2] and yet we still use them. (There is evidence that the SAT II, which measures ability in specific subject areas, does have validity.) Nevertheless, our interviewees are all certain that their primary responsibility is meeting academic goals. They just don't see room for a separate curriculum for SEL.

The solution they *would* accept is infusing social and emotional instruction into academic subjects. This is especially true if it can be done without losing instructional time and without tedious preparation. There is growing agreement on embedding SEL into the general curriculum, for its own sake, and for the many ways it facilitates AL. For example, research by the influential Collaborative for Academic, Social, and Emotional Learning (CASEL) has found that there are average gains of from 11 to 17% in AL when it is blended with SEL.[3] As the new *Guide to SEL Programs Studies*,[4] also by CASEL, puts it:

> Social and emotional learning can serve as an organizing principle for *coordinating all of a school's academic, youth development, and prevention activities*.
>
> [italics ours]

Criteria for Our Strategies

For SEL strategies to be integrated into AL, even if only from time to time, several criteria must be met:

- *Teachers are busy*. AL/SEL lessons must be well organized and easy to implement. Assuming that all teachers already know the AL part of their curriculum, the SEL strategies in our lessons should require no more than 30 minutes of preparation time.
- SEL must not interfere with academic learning (remember, SEL typically *improves* academic scores by between 11 and 17%).
- The relevancy of SEL to the required academic objectives must be apparent to the teacher (and to student teachers).[5] Today, learning standards vary from school to school, state to state, and country to country. However, the three most popular are the Common Core State Standards[6] (CCSS), the International Baccalaureate[7] (IB) standards, and the Next Generation Science Standards[8] (NGSS). We have paraphrased AL goals in each of our lessons based on these

three rather similar international standards because we know you are getting students ready for the globally interconnected world in which they will live.
- SEL must promote an atmosphere that fosters creativity, cooperation, concentration, and critical thinking.
- The strategy should include only the subject matter for which all students are tested and Science (including psychology), Technology, Engineering, the Arts, and Math (STEAM).

This book meets all these criteria, and to date, it is the only resource that does.

Format of This Book

Our book has the following features:

- All Reproducibles will appear on the book's website, where they may be easily downloaded or printed out in multiple copies. The URL for our website is found at www.routledge.com/9781138632066.
- Each of the SEL lessons are closely integrated with a typical learning goal. For example, when summarizing data, pupils document their own pulse rates as an indicator of math anxiety three times a day and for two school weeks (i.e., 15 times). Simple graphs of these data are drawn so that students may look for causal relationships. Experiences known to reduce problems such as test anxiety are also taught (see Chapter 4).
- This book has an international orientation, with a variety of cultural examples.

Format of Each of the Strategies

In each of our strategies, we describe seven elements:

- *Number and name of strategy* (e.g., **2A Math Confidence**)
- *Academic goal by area covered* (language arts, science, and mathematics ELA; STEAM)
- *SEL goal by area covered* (one of the eight 6Seconds strategies based originally on the five CASEL areas: self-awareness,

self-management, social awareness, relationship skills, and responsible decision-making
- *Materials needed* (e.g., **Reproducible 5B1: Sharing Tough Situations**)
- *Engage* (What exactly is the information being presented in this activity?)
- *Activate* (What does it mean to students?)
- *Reflect* (What do they want to do about it?)

These last three elements are also used in the excellent 6Seconds Model.[9]

No doubt about it, new ways of providing SEL are coming to families, to businesses, to entertainment (especially gaming), and to education at all levels.[10] As you know, you are a member of one of the finest professions there is. Since you are reading this, you are probably one of the most dedicated members of that profession. We sincerely hope our book helps you to be even better at attaining your lofty goals.

Notes

1. Dacey, Devlin and Criscitiello, C1 RealTeachIntro, 7/29/2017.
2. Paulos, July 2016.
3. CASEL, 2016.
4. CASEL, 2016, p. 1.
5. Cressey, et al., 2017.
6. www.corestandards.org/
7. www.ibo.org/
8. www.nextgenscience.org/
9. 6Seconds.org, 2016.
10. Transforming Education, 2017.

Part I
Self-Awareness

2

Be Authentic

> Man sacrifices his health in order to make money. Then he sacrifices money to recuperate his health. And then he is so anxious about the future that he does not enjoy the present; the result being that he does not live in the present or the future; he lives as if he is never going to die, and then dies having never really lived.
> —H. H., The Dalai Lama

The 12 traits we espouse in this book are essential to every student's success in life. However, if we had to pick just one, it would be authenticity. Without it, you cannot be a person of character, of integrity. This most important virtue is also about being humble. Humility does not mean being debased or self-degraded. It means "being right-sized," which has two components:

- Authentic persons are objectively aware of their own strengths and weaknesses.
- They don't pretend to be someone they aren't.

Authenticity is central to being comfortable with oneself, to being trusted by friends, and to being a leader.

There Is Teaching, and Then There's *Real Teaching*

> Every teacher has seen this happen: you spend hours making corrections on students' work, only to see identical mistakes on the next assignment. The result can lead to feelings of frustration and dismay. Years ago, when I became the supervising teacher for the school literary magazine, I was amazed by the writing growth I saw in my students. What made such a difference?

Students were doing real work for a real audience, and they wanted to do well. Students had a choice in the type of assignments they had. And they were truly responsible for their work. In my typical English class, if students didn't do their work, they would get a poor grade and both of us would likely feel defeated. But on the magazine staff, if they didn't do the work, someone else would have to do it. After all, no publication leaves a big blank space that says, "Jim didn't finish his story."

I now see that the factors that led to my students' greater academic success are the same ones advocated for in *11 Principles of Effective Character Education*:[1] You do the best you can, and then get honest feedback. We tell our students all the time: "Don't just say 'I like it!' Be kind, but be honest!"

—Lindsey Neves[2]

Real vs. Ideal Self

Psychologist Carl Rogers offered a good insight into authenticity, and his theory underlies our strategies. He said that everyone has two images of themselves:

- Their *ideal self*, which is comprised of all the traits they believe they possess.
- Their *real self*, which is comprised of all the traits they actually have.

Rogers' insight was that the greater the distance between the two, the greater the inner conflict the person suffers. There is a "war" being carried out in the psyche of the conflicted person, which makes it harder for him[3] to be authentic. Such a person lacks self-knowledge, and therefore the power he needs to

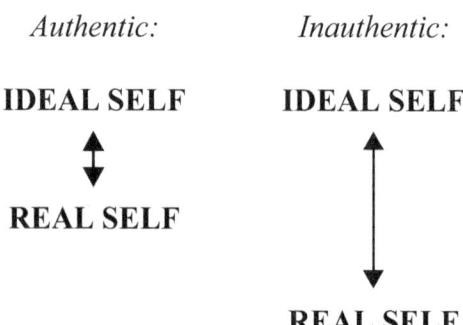

Figure 2.1 The Average Distance between the Real and Ideal Selves

be all he can be. He cannot be trustworthy, and others know it. Undoubtedly, you have seen the implications of this disconnect in the classroom—students who struggle when working in groups or react inappropriately to the slightest hint of criticism. Personalities, in general, fall into two ends of the authenticity continuum:

When the distance between the ideal self and the real self is great, Rogers recommended three possible remedies:

- Lower your ideal expectations to a more reasonable level.
- Raise your real efforts to a more reasonable level.
- And (usually), both.

Knowing and showing yourself accurately is essential to being authentic, a person of character. In your classroom, authenticity leads to intrinsic motivation, which then leads to greater engagement.

Are today's youth learning to become people of character? Here's what *New York Times* editorialist David Brooks, who also teaches a course on character at Yale, wrote recently:

> When it comes to character and virtue, young people have been left on their own. Today's go-getter parents and today's educational institutions work frantically to cultivate neural synapses, to foster good study skills, to promote musical talents. We spend huge amounts of money on safety equipment and sports coaching. We sermonize about the evils of drunk driving. We expend enormous energy guiding and regulating their lives. But when it comes to character and virtue, the most mysterious area of all, suddenly the laissez-faire ethic rules: You're on your own, Jack and Jill; go figure out what is true and just for yourselves.[4]

ACTIVITY 2A What a Hero!

AL Goal: ELA[5] Recount a story, including fables, folktales, and myths from diverse cultures; determine the central moral lesson.

SEL Goal: Self-management Establishing ideals that can motivate greater achievement, especially when the going gets tough.

Materials Needed: pencil and paper; **Reproducible 2A1: Malala Yousafzai: "The Bravest Girl in the World"**

Malala Yousafzai: "The Bravest Girl in the World"

Malala was a 12-year-old student attending a Pakistani school when she wrote a blog for the BBC television network. She supported the rights of girls in her country to an education, even though the ruling Taliban had banned females from attending school. As Malala gained prominence for her writing, South African Bishop Desmond Tutu nominated her for the International Children's Peace Prize.

In October of 2012, a Taliban gunman boarded her school bus and shot her three times in the face. She was in critical condition for days but improved enough to continue her recovery and rehabilitation in England. The Taliban continued with their threats to kill her and her father, but she would not cease to speak out for her young sisters throughout southern Asia. On December 16, 2014, the day of an attack on a military school in Pakistan by the Taliban that claimed 141 lives, the great majority of them children, she said she was "heartbroken over this cowardly act."

Malala's bravery and activism for women's right to education has brought support from all over the world. A UN petition, "I am Malala," was born. The petition's focus was for all children worldwide to have the right to be educated in school by December 2015. The initiative led to the ratification of Pakistan's first "Right to Education Bill." She has been recognized with over 30 distinguished honors and awards from many countries, including being the youngest winner ever of the Nobel Peace Prize in 2014.

Engage:[6] Tell your students that a hero is someone to admire. They may not have met this person, but they know it is someone really special. This is a person they hope to grow up and be like. Ask students if they can tell you the name of such a person. If they don't have a hero now, ask them to consider one: Malala Yousafzai. Read or pass out **Reproducible 2A1: Malala Yousafzai: "The Bravest Girl in the World"**

Activate: Require each of your students to write down if they strongly agree, agree, disagree, or strongly disagree with the following questions about their own personality traits. Are they:

- Courageous, in some areas?
- In control of their lives?
- A leader (in some areas)?
- Patient?
- Kind?

Reflect: Now, ask students to look over their answers in small groups and see what each one of them reveals:

- How is Malala like or different from them?
- Does it make any difference that she is a girl?
- Do they know anyone like her (older or younger)?
- What could they do to be as authentic as she clearly is?

ACTIVITY 2B Behind the Classroom Door

AL Goal: STEAM (Psychological) Develop an objective understanding of one's own personal traits.

SEL Goal: Self-Awareness Introduce children to thinking about who they are, through a projective method.

Most preteen students have only begun to be self-aware. This strategy provides them with a means of thinking about who they are without the usual influences of pride or defensiveness. The technique is called "projection": stating what you really think about a subject without being aware you're doing it.

Materials Needed: paper and pencil

Engage: Suggest to each of your students that he imagine himself standing in a classroom, behind an open door. Tell him to imagine that a small group of his friends is standing out in the hallway. "You can hear them talking about you, but they don't know you're nearby. One of those friends says, 'I really like [your name] because he's so . . . [smart? cute? kind?]'

Each student should write down their name and their answer to this question on paper, privately. Now ask the class to suppose another member of the group in the hall says, "Well, there is one thing I think is not so great about [your name] . . ." Ask each student in your class what he thinks that person is probably saying about him. Repeat this same sequence of these two questions two more times, so each of your pupils will have six words, three positive and three negative, describing themselves. The papers should be turned in to you so you can evaluate the answers in terms of both academic and SEL goals.

Activate: For each of the three positive and three negative adjectives students wrote on their papers, ask them to say why they think that adjective was applied to them ["Because it's true? Because she likes me? Because he's lying?"]. Also ask which of the six adjectives really are true and whether it hurt their feelings to "hear" the negative remarks.

Reflect: Now ask each of your students to think about the following questions without having to write anything down. They might discuss their answers in small groups:

- Would you like everyone to know about the good things those friends said about you?
- How would you feel if everyone knew the bad things they said about you? Do you think it's good for people to know everything about you, even if some of those things hurt your feelings? Why or why not?

Mention Dacey's Law: "Do not worry what people are thinking about you—they aren't!"

ACTIVITY 2C King of the Birds

AL Goal: Literacy Refer to details and examples in a text when explaining what the text says explicitly and when drawing inferences from the text.

SEL Goal: Social Awareness Learn that remembering key details in a situation depends greatly on one's expectations about that situation.

Materials Needed: paper and pencil; **Reproducible 2C1: Common Myth about Birds**[7]

REPRODUCIBLE 2C1

Common Myth about Birds

On an early spring day when the earth was still young, many birds were gathered around an opening in the forest. Suddenly one of the most beautiful of the birds, a bald eagle, flew to a high branch in a tree and called for everyone's attention. Eagle said, "I can see that we are all getting along with each other very well, but we are in danger of attacks. I am fearful that the other animals will try to hurt us if we don't get united behind a strong leader. That is why I think we really need to choose a king. As you can see, I am one of the most powerful of the birds, and so I think I would be the best choice to be king." Then Owl spoke up: "Power is important, but wisdom is even more important. It is well known that I am the wisest of all the birds, so I think I should become the king." Owl was also standing on the high branch, and he puffed out his chest and began strutting around, acting like a king.

Stork flew over and bumped Owl, sending him tumbling. "Listen, Buddy," Stork said angrily. "I bring babies to people. Without me, there wouldn't be any people. Since people are really important, that makes me important too; I think I should be the king of the birds!" Mocking Bird shouted, "I can imitate the songs of 47 different birds. People love birds because of our songs. Who was the best singer? That would be me! Therefore, we really have to choose me for king." "Wait a minute," called Lady Cardinal. "So far you're assuming that the king has to be a male. I am angry that you are excluding females from your thinking!"

"Okay, I have it," said Eagle. "There's only one way to settle this: the bird that can fly the highest will be the king." The biggest and strongest birds thought this was a great idea. The smaller birds were very upset about it, but their voices were so soft that nobody heard. No one noticed what Wren did, either. Very quietly, Wren snuggled her way into the thick feathers of Eagle's shoulder. Even Eagle was not aware of it. Owl said, "When I say go, fly as high as you can." The race to go high was very close at first. Gradually, the big birds became exhausted and had to drop down.

All except for Eagle, that is. He kept flying a little higher, and when he was exhausted, he thought, "I am so happy! I am so tired I can't fly another stroke. Now I will be king!" As he turned to descend, Wren jumped out from her hiding place

© 2018, Taylor & Francis, *Integrating SEL into Your Curriculum*,
John Dacey, Gian Criscitiello, and Maureen Devlin

and flew up a couple of more feet into the sky. When she finally flew down to the ground, she said, "I flew higher than anyone!" She was dismayed to find that the other birds would not accept her as King. They were very angry that she had used this trick to win. They went after her, so she flew deep into the forest, and to this day, she flits from tree to tree, never staying long enough to be caught. All the birds voted that there was no winner, so even now they do not have a king!

Engage: Tell your students that in a moment you will be reading or passing out a story for them, and you have some different listening expectations for each of them. Pass out **Reproducible 2C1: Common Myth about Birds**. After the story they are to record as many of the items as they remember. Have your students count off in threes. Then inform them that the "**ones**" should listen for as many **actions** that the characters do in the story. Give examples of verbs/actions that characters might engage in (e.g., running, falling, jumping, etc.). The "**twos**" should listen to all of the different **feelings** expressed by the characters in the story. Give examples of feelings that characters might have (e.g., sadness, frustration, annoyance, etc.). The "**threes**" should listen for any interactions between the characters in the story. Explain that in a story, characters interact with each other, and it usually happens when they are together. Now read aloud or pass out **Reproducible 2C1: Common Myth about Birds**. Ask your students if someone could summarize what the story is about. Why do they think the birds were unable to select the king?

Activate: 1. Your students need to recognize that their expectations will have a powerful effect on what they remember. Have each student in each group write down what they remember from the story that they were assigned to pay attention to. Ask each student in group **one** to tell you the total number of items on their list. Write these on the board, add them up, and divide by the number of students. This yields the average number of observations made by this group. Do the same thing for groups **two** and **three**, then inform students of the results without sharing the actual actions, feelings, or interactions.

2. Now ask group **one** to write down the feelings the birds had. Ask group **two** to make notes about any interactions between the birds they can remember. Finally, ask group **three** to write down all of the actions that they remember from the story.

3. Make the same calculations for these results that you did in step 1 above. Almost certainly, you will find these numbers to be smaller. This is because students were not expecting to have to answer these questions, and so they will not do as well.

Reflect: Ask the children to explain why their memory was not as good on the second round. Someone will say that they didn't know they were supposed to remember those things too. Ask them to suggest reasons why that should be. Guide them to recognize that this sort of thing happens all the time.

Describe how what we expect to hear will influence what we actually do hear. We should be cautious about how much faith we place in our memories, because they are often influenced greatly by our expectations. When we try to understand ourselves, we usually do so with distorted data. We should always be cautious about just how true our memories are!

ACTIVITY 2D My Personal Shield

AL Goal: STEAM (Psychology, Art) Generate and compare multiple possible solutions to problems; use drawings to symbolize personal attributes.

SEL Goal: Self-Awareness Seek to build a better understanding of one's own personal traits.

Materials Needed: pencil and paper; **Reproducible 2D1: Personal Family Shields; Reproducible 2D2: Personal Shield Blank**

REPRODUCIBLE 2D1

Personal Family Shields

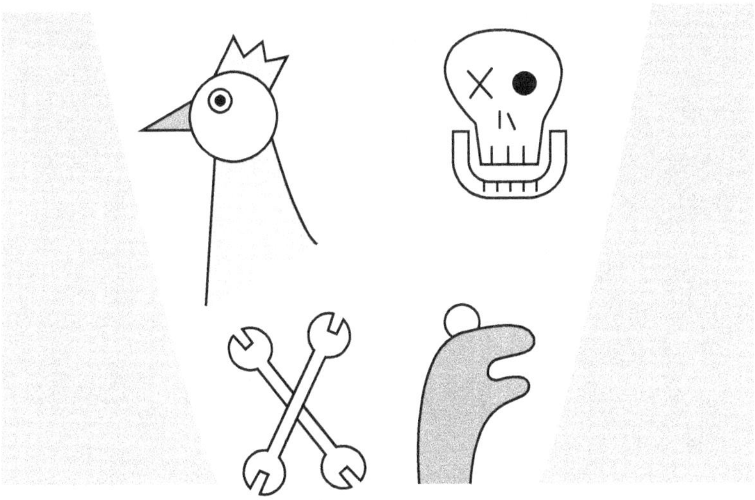

© 2018, Taylor & Francis, *Integrating SEL into Your Curriculum*,
John Dacey, Gian Criscitiello, and Maureen Devlin

REPRODUCIBLE 2D2

Personal Shield Blank

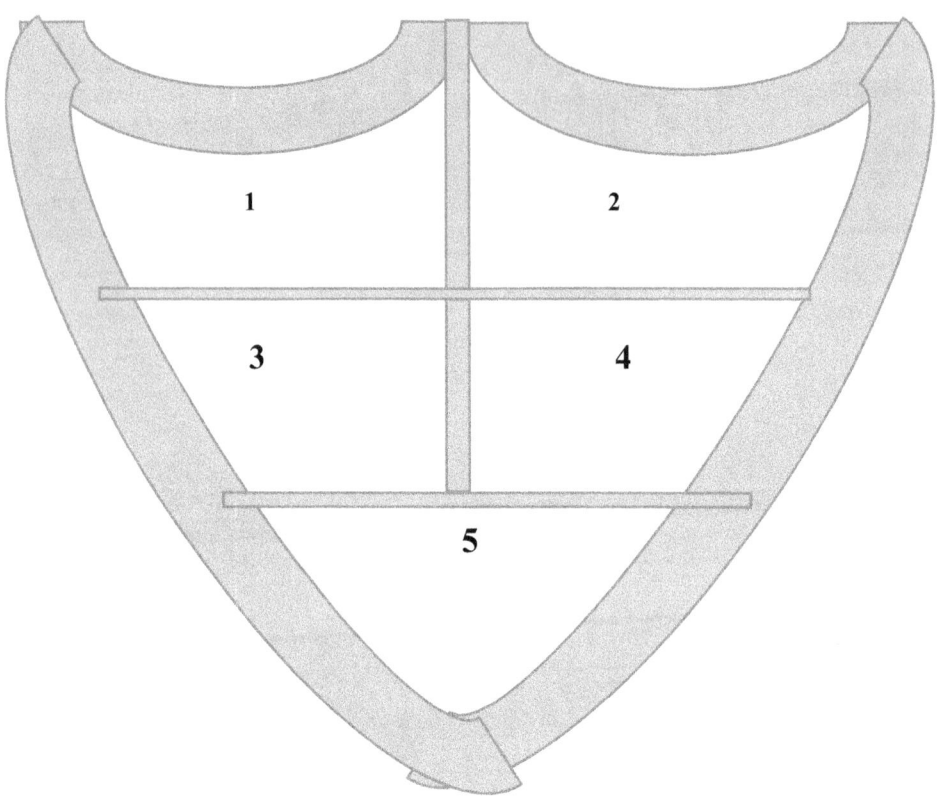

© 2018, Taylor & Francis, *Integrating SEL into Your Curriculum*,
John Dacey, Gian Criscitiello, and Maureen Devlin

Engage: Show the class the example of a real family shield and a whimsical one (**Reproducible 2D1: Personal Family Shields**). Ask for guesses about why some people like to have such a shield. [In the traditions of England and Scotland, a shield or crest refers to the individual's "coat of arms." This artwork appears on a shield. This individual was typically a knight of the realm, and the shield celebrated his achievements through symbols, such as a lion.]

Activate: Now, pass out copies of the shield presented in **Reproducible 2D2: Personal Shield Blank**. They should draw symbols in each of the five sections of the shield that represent their answer to the questions listed below:

1. What is a symbol that stands for a skill you are really good at? [For example, if a student thinks he is a good tennis player, he might draw a tennis racket or a tennis ball or a tennis net.]
2. What is a symbol that stands for a skill that you are really bad at?
3. What is a symbol that stands for the personality trait that shows what a good person you are? [An example might be the trait of kindness, the symbol might be of a stick figure who is crying, and another stick figure putting her arm around him.]
4. What is a symbol that stands for the personality trait that shows that you are not such a good person?
5. What is a symbol that could stand for who you are as a whole person, that would represent the total view of you to the world? [For instance, the picture might be of the person standing on the stage with lots of stick figures in the audience applauding.]

Reflect: Form groups of four. Instruct students to show their shield, one at a time, to the other three, who try to guess what the icons on the shield stand for. When each student has related the meaning of his symbols, you might have each of them write a brief paragraph or two about how this exercise made them feel.

If you feel comfortable doing so, you might ask the students in each group if what they heard seems true to them. This will allow each shield-maker to get important feedback from others about the truth of what they see in themselves. The potential for seriously hurt feelings is obvious, however, so you will have to do what you think is right about this suggestion.

ACTIVITY 2E The Prideful Pig

AL Goal: Literacy Make connections between the text of a story or drama and a visual or oral presentation of the text.

SEL Goal: Self-Awareness Becoming better aware of one's own positive and negative traits.

This strategy for teaching humility is about being "right-sized," that is, having the correct assessment of our true selves. This lesson will help your students think about what that means.

Materials Needed: paper and drawing mediums (crayons, markers, or paint); **Reproducible 2E1: Two Pigs**; **Reproducible 2E2: Drawing of a Pig**

REPRODUCIBLE 2E1

Two Pigs

What distinguishes a proud *pig* from a humble "right-sized" pig?

© 2018, Taylor & Francis, *Integrating SEL into Your Curriculum*,
John Dacey, Gian Criscitiello, and Maureen Devlin

REPRODUCIBLE 2E2

Drawing of a Pig

© 2018, Taylor & Francis, *Integrating SEL into Your Curriculum*,
John Dacey, Gian Criscitiello, and Maureen Devlin

Engage: Show the class the drawing in **Reproducible 2E1: Two Pigs**. Explain the difference. Now let them see **Reproducible 2E2: Drawing of a Pig**. They can use that for a model of a pig.

Activate: Tell your students to draw a picture of two pigs, sort of like the pigs you have just shown them. One is a proud pig and the other is a right-sized pig.

The proud pig might have a big head, a little heart, and an upturned snout because he doesn't care about anyone but himself. He might wear fancy shoes, etc. The right-sized pig might have a big heart, big ears (for hearing about others' needs), and long legs with big muscles for helping others.

Reflect: Ask your students:

1. In what other ways could you show that the second pig is right-sized?
2. Do you think that you are right-sized? How can you tell? In what ways do you show the true you to others?
3. What are three strengths that you have?
4. What are three challenges you face with regard to being right-sized?
5. You may want to write a "snapshot" or "small moment" story to describe this event in your life, or perhaps you will write a fictional story that draws from your experience with made-up characters such as the proud and humble pigs we began the lesson with.

You (the teacher) might want to look into whole programs designed for classrooms to enhance authenticity. You will find their names on our website. With this and all the applications you will find in this book, do your best to evoke meaningful discussion, being a good listener as much as possible. Can you see how this strategy fits the overall objectives of SEL (and AL)? Would you agree that preparation for this type of lesson is not too demanding of your time? Is it worth the trouble?

Notes

1 Petersen, 2012.
2 Lindsey Neves, Sixth grade teacher in N. Attleboro, MA, personal communication.
3 In an effort to resolve the gender problem, we use the female pronoun in odd-numbered chapters and the male pronoun in even-numbered chapters.

4 Brooks, 2014.
5 We assume teachers know how to teach this material, and so will have little or nothing to say about academic learning (AL) goals.
6 The last three sections of all of our activities are entitled *"Engage," "Activate,"* and *"Reflect."* These sections coincide with the activities offered at 6Seconds.org, an organization we recommend to teachers who want to learn more about SEL best practices.
7 This myth is told among many native peoples.

3

Practice Mindfulness

Be happy in the moment, that's enough. Each moment is all we need, not more.
—Mother Teresa

The present moment is filled with joy and happiness. If you are attentive, you will see it.
—Thich Nhat Hanh

The concept of mindfulness is not new. Meditation, for instance, is ancient, but recent research has improved our grasp of its uses. The father of research on mindfulness, psychiatrist John Kabat-Zinn, says it is "the awareness that emerges through paying attention on purpose, in the present moment, and nonjudgmentally to the unfolding of experience."[1] Most of us, he says, miss all kinds of important information about ourselves as well as others. We lack awareness.

Psychologist Ellen Langer, says that the *unmindful* person is one who *"is often in error, but seldom in doubt."*[2] This is because that individual has come to believe most of the information she has is unquestionably true, and therefore she no longer needs to pay it any mind. The essence of mindfulness, however, is paying attention.

At least eight advantages to being mindful of one's health have been documented.[3] It can:

- Enhance brain performance.
- Promote creative thinking.

- Alleviate stress.
- Curtail anxiety.
- Increase compassion.
- Decrease depression.
- Minimize chronic pain.
- Lower risk of heart attack or stroke.

ACTIVITY 3A Just Breathe . . .

AL Goal: STEAM (Biological Science—respiratory system)

SEL Goal: Self-Awareness To practice mindfulness by focusing on a vital process that happens numerous times each minute.

Materials Needed: **Reproducible 3A1: Guided Breathing Technique**

REPRODUCIBLE 3A1

Guided Breathing Technique

1. Find a comfortable position. You may feel relaxed sitting in a chair or lying flat on the floor. Take a moment to get comfortable—find a position that feels good to you. Close your eyes. Notice where your body is touching the chair [or the floor]. Pay attention to your hands in your lap [or by your sides on the floor]. As you rest comfortably, notice what you're feeling in your body. Start with your toes and work your way up your legs; past your knees and thighs; past your hips, stomach, and back; along your arms; across your shoulders; up the back of your neck and to the top of your head. Observe the muscles in your face, and just . . . breathe.

2. Now take a deep breath through your mouth and then exhale slowly through your nose or mouth, noticing the sensation as the air enters and leaves your body. Notice the air as it enters your mouth—is it cool? Warm? Where do you feel the air? Do you feel it inside your nostrils? On the back of your throat? Notice your stomach rising and falling with your breaths. You might place one or both hands on your tummy to feel it rise and fall with each breath.

3. As you pay attention to the in and out breath, you might notice thoughts entering your mind. You might notice feelings in parts of your body. Now bring your attention back to your breath. Continue the breathing for approximately 3 minutes.

© 2018, Taylor & Francis, *Integrating SEL into Your Curriculum*,
John Dacey, Gian Criscitiello, and Maureen Devlin

Engage: Tell students that they are going to take a few moments to just . . . breathe. Breathing is extraordinary because often we don't notice it happening since breathing is automatic. During most of the many breaths we take each day, we are focused on something else in our busy lives. Breathing is a natural connection between your body and your mind. When we take time to focus on our breath, we begin to notice the present moment in a clear, calm, and focused way.

Now slowly read **Reproducible 3A1: Guided Breathing Technique** to students.

Activate: After the exercise, debrief with students about what they noticed or wondered about.

- How did you feel before you started this breathing exercise?
- How do you feel afterwards?
- What parts of your body did you become aware of during the exercise?

Reflect: Now ask for these conclusions:

- Is this a part of your body that you usually pay attention to?
- Did other thoughts enter your mind during the exercise?
- Did you notice anything about yourself that you've never paid attention to before?
- Was this exercise useful to you? How so?

ACTIVITY 3B Color the Pain Away

AL Goal: STEAM (Biology, Psychology) How the body deals with pain.

SEL Goal: *Self-Awareness* Demonstrate the practical usefulness of mindfulness in dealing with pain.

Materials Needed: none

Engage: Tell the class that mindfulness has many very practical uses. It can help diminish pain. Pain happens to us all the time, unfortunately, and learning ways to think about it is helpful. Say that "the nerves in your body send a message to the pain center in your brain, which reacts to protect you when you've hurt yourself. Many times, however, the pain is not useful, and you want it to go away."

Activate: Ask students to remember a time recently when they were in pain. This can be a physical or emotional discomfort. Tell them to focus on the pain itself rather than the circumstances when they experienced the pain. Tell them to focus on the part of their body where the pain was. Now imagine that that part is red—fiery red! Have them look at the part in their mind's eye for a few moments and now notice that the part is starting to turn yellow. As it goes from red to yellow, it doesn't hurt as much. Now see it as white. Even less pain. Now blue. Even less pain. And finally, see the part as green. It is calm and pain free.

Reflect: Have the students discuss what they noticed during this activity.

- When they thought of the pain as the color red, how did it feel?
- Did the memory of the pain lessen as they went through the color changes?
- When they saw the pain as the color green, how did it feel?

Explain that if they saw a positive difference in how the memory of the past pain felt, they should see a difference the next time they experience real pain. Remind them to try picturing it in this series of colors, and they'll be amazed at how quickly it calms down and hurts less.

ACTIVITY 3C Your Feelings Thermometer

AL Goal: STEAM Become familiar with relative reading on a thermometer.

SEL Goal: Self-Awareness Pay attention to the messages our bodies are telling us.

Materials Needed: **Reproducible 3C1: Drawing or Photo of a Thermometer**

REPRODUCIBLE 3C1

Drawing or Photo of a Thermometer

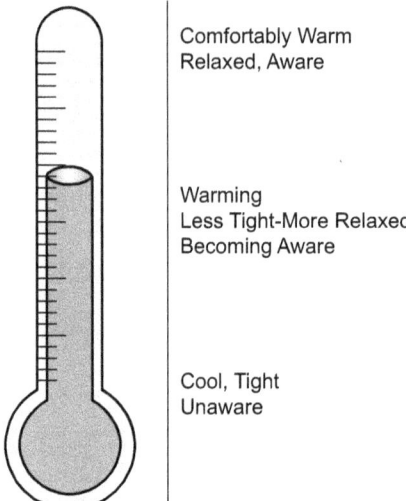

© 2018, Taylor & Francis, *Integrating SEL into Your Curriculum*,
John Dacey, Gian Criscitiello, and Maureen Devlin

Engage: Tell students that there are many tools used to measure different things in science. We use thermometers to measure the temperature of the air—either outside or inside. We can also use a thermometer to measure the temperature of liquids and solids. The information we get from thermometers can tell us how things are going within and around what we are measuring. Our bodies can tell us how we are feeling in a way that is very similar to a thermometer. Show them **Reproducible 3C1: Drawing or Photo of a Thermometer**.

Activate: Tell the students they are going to take the "feelings temperature" of one part of their body. Tell them to choose a part of their body—perhaps their neck, shoulder, stomach, head—any part of their body they choose. Have them bring their attention to feeling that part. Ask them to record on their thermometer worksheet a "feelings temperature." Tell them that as they breathe, they should imagine that they are breathing into that part of their body.

As they pay attention to their body part, they may notice that the sensation starts to change a little. Their muscles might begin to relax, and they may notice warmth or coldness in that part of their body.

Reflect: Have the students record the "feeling temperature" of their body part after trying to change its temperature.

- Did they notice any change?
- If yes, what kind of change happened—a positive or negative difference?
- How does the temperature of their body part compare to their overall feeling?
- Did they notice anything else about their feelings during the exercise?

ACTIVITY 3D Where the Numbers Are

AL Goal: STEAM (Number Sense) Become familiar with the sequence of numbers on a number line and identify "friendly" or "landmark" numbers.

SEL Goal: Self-Awareness Practice mindfulness through identifying familiar and unfamiliar thoughts in familiar settings.

Materials Needed: **Reproducible 3D1: Number Lines**; number line from 0 to 10, 0 to 100, 0 to 1,000, etc. (based on student level of understanding)

REPRODUCIBLE 3D1

Number Lines

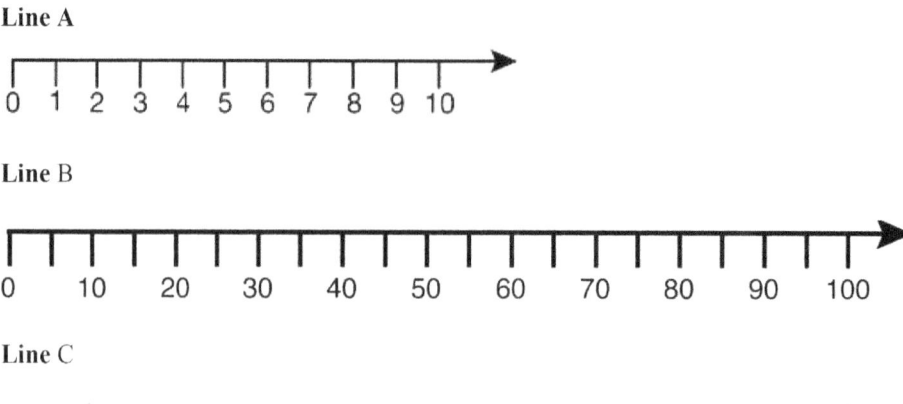

Engage: Tell students that sometimes our thoughts are welcome and serve us well. Other times, our thoughts are not so welcome—they are confusing and keep us from thinking clearly. We wish they would leave, but they just stay put. Imagine that you become so familiar with your thoughts that you can greet them in your mind, much as you would your aunt or a neighbor. You don't need to engage in a conversation with them. Instead, you can simply greet them and then move along just as you might imagine a number line and move from one number to the next.

Activate: Pass out **Reproducible 3D1: Number Lines**

Assign either Line A, B, or C to the students. Ask them to look at that line carefully for a moment. Then have them close their eyes and begin at zero and picture in their minds each number as the number line progresses. They can go up by whatever increment they choose. Have them take a break at "familiar" numbers like 10, 50, 100 and look backwards and then forwards again in their minds. Ask them to continue beyond the ending point of the number line they have. Ask them how far they can go up the number line.

Reflect: Ask these questions:

- How much of the number line extension were they able to picture in their minds?
- Were there any familiar points along the number line that you felt comfortable with?
- Did parts of your mindful number line get confused or blurry?
- Where did that happen? Why did you think it got blurry or unclear at that point?
- How did it make you feel when your mindful number line became blurry?
- How might remembering a past experience be similar and different than imagining the number line?

ACTIVITY 3E In Someone Else's Shoes

AL Goal: Literacy Character analysis—describe a character in a story and her traits, feelings, or motivations.

SEL Goal: Self-Awareness/Social Awareness Learn that empathizing with others can lead to increased understanding of one's self.

Materials Needed: a passage from a current novel that the class is reading or is familiar with, or a passage from a similar piece of literature.

Engage: Many times, children in this age group are able to empathize with others more easily than they are able to empathize or be mindful of their own feelings. This heightened awareness of other people's feelings can help them become aware of their own feelings.

Activate: Read the passage from a book in which they know who the main character is. They will be putting themselves into the shoes of the main character. Ask them to listen carefully and imagine how the main character in the passage may have felt during this part of the story. Have the students record the feelings that the main character experienced.

Reflect: During the discussion afterwards, review the feelings recorded by the students and have them explain why they think the character experienced them. Also ask them what they notice about the feelings. See if there were any differences in the recorded feelings between students and make sure that the students take notice of those differences. Ask students to explain why they may have interpreted the character's feelings differently.

> Explain that each of us reacts differently to any given circumstance. Many of us may have different reactions to the same situation. Have them imagine that they are in the character's shoes, and ask if they would have felt the same way. Why?
>
> Have them turn the tables and imagine a time that was difficult, scary, or exciting for them. What were their feelings as they went through that experience? If the character from the story was in the same situation, how would being able to pay attention to her feelings and thoughts help her get through the situation?

The child who is mindful will be better able to remain calm in the face of stressful situations. Mindfulness is an SEL skill that contributes to all the others.

Notes

1 Kabat-Zinn, 2013.
2 Langer, December 5, 2014.
3 Bergland, 2016.

Part II
Self-Management

4

Think Positively

Once you replace negative thoughts with positive ones, you'll start having positive results.

—Willie Nelson

"Rachel" was attempting vainly to stuff her books, folders, and notebooks into the metal pocket under her desk. Miss Neves had told the students to create a "nice clean space" on their desktops. The instructions that she was about to give would help prepare them for the state test that would occur in four months. The date is a looming presence that all teachers feel—in the lunchroom, in the copy room, in meetings, in articles on the internet. "Hurry up! Get into these kids' heads! Make it work!"

Rachel kept shoving. Students were starting to look at her. The classroom atmosphere was becoming overwrought. Softly, Miss Neves told her to put the books on the floor. Rachel threw her hands in the air, stomped her feet, and began to sob. "I just can't! I can't make it fit!" Rachel was obviously struggling to cope with a disappointing outcome, and here Miss Neves was insisting that she create a "nice, clean space."

—Lindsey Neves[1]

Can you relate to this new teacher's feelings? Students are not the only ones in your classroom who experience the effects of stress, right? Resiliency in the face of stress is one of the most desirable traits in the SEL pantheon because stressful situations are so common these days (see Chapter 7). If a child's stress level is high, or even moderate, *that child cannot think well*.

You know you cannot control what happens in your students' lives outside the classroom (one of the most difficult realities for us to accept). However, "many studies show that [elementary pupils can] cope with anxiety. When asked how they deal with the fear of receiving a needle from the doctor, they suggest thinking of a happy time, such as eating ice cream."[2] This is known as "positive thinking." As expert Nira Datta states, there are several relevant facts you need to know:

- Children as young as five are able to grasp the principles of positive thinking.
- Children get better at understanding positive thinking as they get older.
- When it is nurtured, positive thinking is a powerful coping tool and helps build resilience in a child.
- Students should always acknowledge a negative situation or feeling. Then you can help them see their problem in a way that is positive and productive.[3]

It is clear that you can infuse SEL into your lessons such that your students learn to think and feel more positively as they try to achieve your school's academic goals.

The activity below is about serious anxiety and sadness (depression). The ones that follow are all about anxiety. We choose this imbalance because, by and large, classroom teachers can ameliorate anxiety more easily than they can depression or anger. The latter two may be more life-threatening, and often require medication as well as psychotherapy.

ACTIVITY 4A Understanding O. Henry's *The Last Leaf*

AL Goal: Literacy Interpret underlying meaning of a symbolic masterpiece.

SEL Goal: Self-Awareness Recognize the connection between thoughts, overall mental attitude, and actions.

Materials Needed: **Reproducible 4A1**: ***The Last Leaf*, by O. Henry** (slightly edited to fit preteen ability)

REPRODUCIBLE 4A1

The Last Leaf, by O. Henry

At the top of a squatty, three-story brick building, Sue and Johnsy had their art studio. "Johnsy" was Sue's nickname for Joanna. In November an illness the doctors called pneumonia came to the neighborhood, Johnsy was one of the first to catch it. She lay scarcely moving on her bed, looking through the small window panes at the side of the next brick house. One morning the busy doctor examined her, then invited her friend Sue into the hallway. "She has one chance in ten," he said, as he put away his thermometer. "And that chance is for her to want to live. Your friend has made up her mind that she's not going to get well. I will do all that medicine can accomplish. However, she needs to commit to living!"

Sue went into the bedroom, and looked at Johnsy, who lay with her face toward the window. Johnsy's eyes were open wide. She was counting backward. "Twelve," she said, and a little later "eleven"; and then "ten," and "nine"; and then "eight" and "seven," almost together.

Sue looked out the window. There she saw an old, old ivy vine, which climbed half way up the brick wall. The wind had been ripping its leaves from the vine until its branches clung, almost bare, to the crumbling bricks. "What is it, dear? Tell me," said Sue. "Leaves," Johnsy replied. "On the ivy vine. When the last one falls I must die, too. I've known that for three days. Didn't the doctor tell you?"

"Oh, I never heard of such nonsense," said Sue, in a voice full of scorn. "What have old ivy leaves to do with your getting well? And you used to love that vine so, you naughty girl. Don't be a goose. Why, the doctor told me this morning that your chances for getting well real soon were ten to one! Try to take some broth now."

"There goes another," said Johnsy, keeping her eyes fixed on the window. "No, I don't want any broth. That leaves just four. I want to see the last one fall before it gets dark. Then I'll go too."

"Johnsy, dear," said Sue, bending over her, "Will you promise me to keep your eyes closed, and not look out the window? Besides, I don't want you to keep looking at those silly ivy leaves."

Johnsy, closing her eyes, said, "I want to see the last one fall. I'm tired of waiting. I'm tired of thinking. I want to turn loose my hold on everything, and go sailing down, down, just like one of those poor, tired leaves."

© 2018, Taylor & Francis, *Integrating SEL into Your Curriculum*,
John Dacey, Gian Criscitiello, and Maureen Devlin

"Try to sleep," said Sue. "I must call Mr. Behrman up to be my model. I'll not be gone a minute. Don't try to move 'til I come back." Old Mr. Behrman was a painter who lived on the ground floor beneath them. He was past 70 and had a beard curling down from his cheeks. Behrman was a failure in art. Forty years he had painted without having any success. He had been always about to paint a masterpiece, but had never yet begun it. For several years he had painted nothing except now and then a something for advertising. He earned a little by serving as a model to those young artists who could not pay the price of a professional model. He drank to excess, and always talked of his coming masterpiece. He was a fierce little old man, regarding himself as special guardian to protect the two young artists in the studio above.

Sue found Behrman smelling strongly of cheap booze in his dimly lighted den below. In one corner was a blank canvas on an easel that had been waiting there for twenty-five years to receive the first line of the masterpiece. She told him of Johnsy's belief that she would die when the last leaf on the ivy vine outside their building would fall.

Old Behrman, with his red eyes filled with tears, shouted his contempt for such idiotic ideas. "Vat!" he cried. "Is dere people in de world mit der foolishness to die because leafs dey drop off from a confounded vine? I haf not heard of such a thing. No, I will not pose as a model for you. Vy do you allow dot silly idea to come into her brain? Ach, dot poor lettle Miss Yohnsy." "She is very ill and weak," said Sue, "and the fever has left her mind full of strange fancies. Very well, Mr. Behrman, if you do not care to pose for me, you needn't. But I think you are a horrid man!"

When Sue awoke the next morning she found Johnsy with dull, wide-open eyes staring at the drawn green shade. "Pull it up; I want to see," she ordered, in a whisper. Wearily Sue obeyed.

Amazingly, after the beating rain and fierce gusts of wind that had endured through the long night, there yet stood out against the brick wall one ivy leaf. It was the last on the vine. Still dark green near its stem, it hung bravely from a branch some twenty feet above the ground. "It is the last one," said Johnsy. "I thought it would surely fall during the night. I heard the wind. It will fall to-day, and I shall die at the same time."

"Dear, dear!" said Sue, leaning her worn face down to the pillow, "think of me, if you won't think of yourself. What would I do?" But Johnsy did not answer.

The day wore away, and even though the twilight had fallen, they could see the lone ivy leaf clinging to its stem against the wall. And then, with the coming of the

© 2018, Taylor & Francis, *Integrating SEL into Your Curriculum*,
John Dacey, Gian Criscitiello, and Maureen Devlin

night the north wind was again blowing hard. When it was light enough, Johnsy commanded Sue to raise the shade.

The ivy leaf was still there!

Johnsy lay for a long time looking at it. "I've been a bad girl, Sue," said Johnsy. "Something has made that last leaf stay there to show me how wicked I was. It is a sin to want to die. You may bring me a little broth now, and some milk, and-no; bring me a hand-mirror first, and then pack some pillows about me, and I will sit up and watch you cook."

An hour later she said: "Sue, someday I hope to paint the Bay of Naples."

The next day the doctor said to Sue: "She's out of danger. You've won. Nutrition and care now—that's all." And that afternoon Sue came to the bed where Johnsy lay, contentedly knitting a very blue wool shoulder scarf, put one arm around her, pillows and all. "I have something to tell you, my little friend," she said. "Mr. Behrman died of pneumonia today in the hospital. He was ill only two days. The janitor found him on the morning of the first day in his room downstairs helpless with pain. His shoes and clothing were wet through and icy cold. They couldn't imagine where he had been on such a dreadful night. And then they found a lantern, still lighted, and a ladder that had been dragged from its place, and some scattered brushes, and a palette with green and yellow colors mixed on it, and look out the window, dear, at the last ivy leaf on the wall. Didn't you wonder why it never fluttered or moved when the wind blew? Ah, darling, it's Behrman's masterpiece! He painted it there the night the last leaf fell."

Engage: Tell the class that we all experience hardship in our lives at one time or another, whether it is a test on which we didn't do as well as we thought, a sports game that we lost, or the loss of a loved one. Everyone needs to learn how to bounce back from hardship. This is called "grit" or resilience ("grit" is not accepted by some due to racist roots—see Chapter 7). Read or pass out **Reproducible 4A1:** *The Last Leaf,* **by O. Henry** and inform them that this story has one person who just wants to quit, and two others who try to think positively.

Activate: Say: "Now that I've read *The Last Leaf* to you, I'd like you to do a Turn and Talk: Turn to a person sitting next to you and share with each other what you remember from this story." Then have the same partners complete this sentence that states the main point:

"The main character, _____ , wanted to _____ , but _____."

Share partners' sentences, and then explain that the sick woman in the story falsely thinks that she is going to die when the last leaf falls. Try to remember a time when you had a false thought that you believed to be true. What was that thought? What did you do about that thought? Could you find a way to think about it more positively?

- Do you think the sick person has a mental problem, in addition to her physical illness? Is she sad or "depressed"? What do you think the word "depressed" means?
- What should you do if you feel frightened (or sad or angry)?
- What do you think it means to be a hero? Is there a hero in this story? Why or why not?
- Do you have a hero? Who is it? If you do not have a hero, should you get one?
- How do we know if someone is feeling sad or depressed? What do you think it feels like in our bodies and minds? What does the word "anxious" mean? When kids feel anxious, how can you tell? What do you think it feels like? How do anxious people act?

Reflect:

- What do you think we can learn from this story?
- Why do you think O. Henry wrote it?

- O. Henry was a very creative writer. Let's try to think like him. Why do you think he wanted to write a story about such a sad person as Johnsy? Is the elderly painter also a sad character?

ACTIVITY 4B Fill the Space around You

AL Goal: STEAM Learn the science behind reducing cortisol level in blood.

SEL Goal: Self-Management Control one's anxious over-reactions to environmental stressors.

Materials Needed: **Reproducible 4B1: Short, Scary Story**

Short, Scary Story

A 10-year-old boy named Jimmy was sitting at the beach with his mother, father, and younger sister Anne. The family decided to go down the beach to the restaurant for lunch, but Jimmy said he wasn't hungry and would rather stay on the blanket. The others left, and after a little while, he got sick of doing that and walked away from the water toward the road. As he neared the road, a yellow limousine pulled up beside him. A man dressed in khakis and a green T-shirt got out of the car and opened the back door. Seated in the back seat was an extremely old man, his face twisted in a hideous smile. The younger man said just two words: "Get in!" Jimmy screamed and ran away as fast as he could. He didn't turn around until he got back to his blanket. The car and the two men were nowhere to be seen.

His family could see that he was upset, but they thought it was probably because they had been gone so long. "I know," said Jimmy's father. "Let's go over to the Ferris wheel and go for a ride." The first person Jimmy saw was the ticket-taker, a young man in khakis and a green T-shirt. "You're next," he said, grinning and pointing to the bucket seat. There sat the old man from the car!

Engage: Tell students this is a strategy they will think must be magic! It has been found that how you sit or lie can greatly affect the "cortisol" level in your blood.[4] Cortisol is a substance that moves through the blood stream and is known as a "hormone." Its presence is the source of most anxiety. For example, it causes some children to worry so much of the time.

Activate: Have students practice taking their pulse for 20 seconds by placing their fingers on the side of their neck and count the number of beats they feel, and writing that number down. Then read the short, scary story in **Reproducible 4B1: Short, Scary Story.** Now tell your students to take their pulse again and write it down. The number should be higher, because their cortisol level has gone up.

Finally tell them, "If you open yourself up by spreading your arms wide, uncrossing your legs, and throwing your head back, like magic you will calm down. Your cortisol level will drop. Your pulse will slow down. Let's see if it works [repeat taking pulse as above]. How many of you got a lower pulse this time? If you have a tightened posture, with your legs crossed, your head forward, and your arms crossed on your chest, cortisol goes back up. Let's test that.

Reflect: It doesn't matter if your mind is the victim of anxious thoughts, you can always use the opening-up method! Remember to use this technique when you start to become frightened, and you will usually be okay.

ACTIVITY 4C Scrunch Those Muscles!

AL Goal: STEAM Learn the science behind reducing lactic acid in muscles.

SEL Goal: Self-Management Relieve anxiety caused by tense muscles. Especially recommended for boys.

Materials Needed: none

Engage: Explain to the class that when we become fearful, nature has arranged for our muscles to become flooded with a substance called "lactic acid." This acid causes our muscles to be tense and ready for the "fight-or-flight" response. This is an ancient tactic built into our brains. When attacked by a sabretooth tiger, you had two choices: try to kill him with your spear, or run away as fast as you can. Today we still have that response when we are frightened, but it doesn't work so well for us. For example, if you're giving a speech on the stage and you find yourself terrified, it doesn't do to scream at the audience to stop looking at you, or to run off the stage.

What we need to do when frightened is to get rid of some of that lactic acid. The only way to flush it out is to tighten all your muscles. We do this by either stretching our muscles (ever notice cats and dogs up from a nap?), or we can tense our muscles as hard as we can.

Activate: Ask the students to try calming their nerves by tensing as many muscles in their entire body as they can. If they are in a public place like school, they will probably want to do this in a more private place (the restroom?), standing or sitting, as they prefer.

But let them practice this at their desks for now. They should start by clenching their fists and flexing their arm muscles. Next they should tighten their leg muscles. Finally, they clench their teeth, their neck, and their abdomen. Finally, maintaining the tension, they take in a deep breath, blow it out forcefully, and then hold their breath for a count of six seconds (say one-Mississippi, two-Mississippi, up to six). Now completely relax. Assume the "open posture" (previous exercise).

Reflect: Notice how your heart has slowed down? Do you feel calmer? Do you think you could do this while sitting at your desk when something is frightening you or causing you stress?

ACTIVITY 4D Drawing Your Fears Away

AL Goal: STEAM Using art to create an emotional response.

SEL Goal: Self-Management Learning to rely on mental imagery to calm fears and anxiety.

Materials Needed: colored pencils; photo of two swans with their heads together (e.g., dreamstime.com/royalty-free-stock-image-two-swans-reflection-image6018286); Ludwig van Beethoven—Symphony No. 6, "Pastoral," 2nd movement (to be shown on whiteboard, full screen): A good example may be found at: youtube.com/watch?v=IoHpMYdTJDQ

REPRODUCIBLE 4D1

Outline of Two Swans

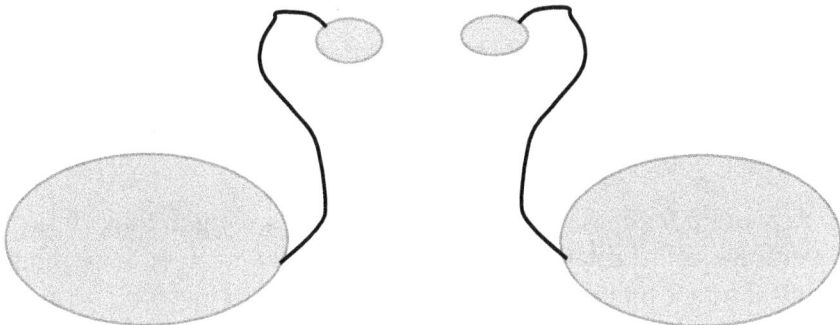

© 2018, Taylor & Francis, *Integrating SEL into Your Curriculum*,
John Dacey, Gian Criscitiello, and Maureen Devlin

Engage: Play the Beethoven piece from his Symphony No. 6. As your students listen to it, show the picture of the two swans with their heads together.

Activate: Ask students to make a drawing of the two swans, beginning with copying the drawing seen in **Reproducible 4D1: Outline of Two Swans**. Using the colored pencils, markers, or crayons, they should elaborate on this simple line drawing until they are satisfied with their picture of the two swans. Ask them to try to associate the music they are hearing with the swans gently floating on a beautiful lake, such as the one seen in the YouTube video you are now playing.

Reflect: Explain to them that they can keep their drawing in their desks, and whenever they feel frightened, they can take it out and try to remember the beautiful music that is now playing. Tell them that just looking at the picture will help them to calm down. Try this just before giving an exam. Give them a few minutes to stare at their drawing, trying to remember how relaxed they felt when they did it. After the test, ask them if it helped.

Stress in Your Classroom

In 1936, Hans Selye (the father of stress research) was studying the endocrine system of cows, which led to the discovery of the "general adaptation syndrome."[5] He described it as a general call to arms of the body's defensive forces. Upon further research, he found that when people (all animals, in fact) experience an initial stressor (a policeman says, "Come with me," for instance), their coping ability (e.g., blood flow to the muscles) suffers. Then, almost immediately, the individual enters a "stage of resistance." In this second stage, an almost complete reversal of the alarm reaction occurs. During this stage, he appears to have adapted successfully to the stressor.

If the stressor continues, however, eventually this leads to a "stage of exhaustion." Now the physiological responses revert to their condition during the stage of alarm. The ability to handle the stress decreases, the level of resistance is lost, and the organism weakens and eventually dies. Here is a diagram of the general adaptation syndrome. From time to time, many of your students fall somewhere on this stress continuum. Do you know which ones?

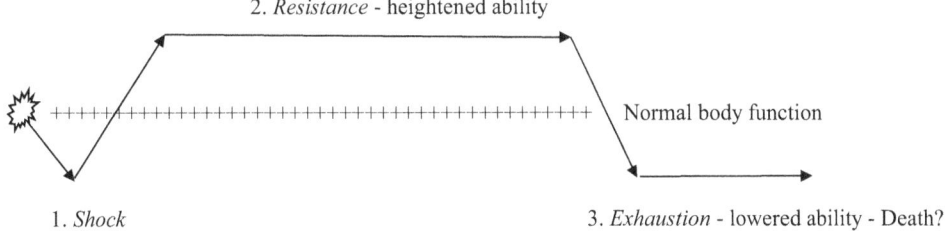

Figure 4.1 The General Adaptation Syndrome

The General Adaptation Syndrome

        ACTIVITY 4E Scientific Measurement of a Body Function

AL Goal: STEAM Compare and contrast the information gained from experiments, in particular, biofeedback.

SEL Goal: Social Awareness Understand the effects of social stimuli on body functions. Biofeedback is a tool that provides data, often electronic, about the human body. The most common indicator is a person's heart rate or pulse, which elevates when the person is under stress. The purpose of biofeedback is to learn how to identify and control thoughts, physical sensations, and behavior. For example, hearing someone shout can be scary to many children. This emotion can quickly turn to a belief that something is seriously wrong, even when nothing is. In this thought pattern, the mind/body connection will likely produce poor concentration and an uncomfortable feeling of tension and foreboding.

Materials Needed: pulse oximeter (on Amazon for $17); **Reproducible 4E1: Tracking Sheet for the Effects of the Situation on Your Pulse Rate**

REPRODUCIBLE 4E1

Tracking Sheet for the Effects of the Situation on Your Pulse Rate

Time of Day	Situation	Starting Pulse Rate	Ending Pulse Rate	Change
Ex.: 8am	First period of class 12/11/16	80	67	−13

© 2018, Taylor & Francis, *Integrating SEL into Your Curriculum*, John Dacey, Gian Criscitiello, and Maureen Devlin

Engage: Of course you could just take a child's pulse using your fingers and the second hand of your watch. However, the power of this instrument comes from a student watching his pulse rate number come down on the oximeter's screen as he uses various calming methods. The oximeter is a simple, portable tool that clips comfortably on a child's fingertip and measures heart rate in real time. This instrument is also available at your local pharmacy or medical supply store for a higher price. Other types of biofeedback machines offer a complex of biological feedback, but they cost much more.

Activate: Pick a student and tell him that you are going to clip this device onto his pointer finger. Tell him to think of a scene from a scary movie. Now ask him to look at his heart rate number on this little monitor, called an "oximeter." Tell him write his pulse rate down on this chart **(Reproducible 4E1: Tracking Sheet for the Effects of the Situation on Your Pulse Rate)**. Now he should to try to control his feelings simply by changing his thoughts. That will make the number in the window on the monitor go down. He should close his eyes, relax, and breathe slowly. (Pause) Don't tell him anything except that his job is to notice his breathing and to think about relaxing. That will lower his heart rate.

After a few moments, have your student open his eyes and read the pulse rate on the oximeter. Almost certainly, it will be a lower number than before. Tell him to record the new number on the tracking sheet. Write down the difference between the two numbers on the sheet and talk about how he feels, physically and emotionally, with a higher versus a lower heart rate. Try this technique again, to see if he can get an even lower number. Students can create a tracking record over days or weeks.

Reflect: Practicing during a relaxed time for a period of a few weeks will help your students learn the effects of biofeedback and understand its value during stressful times. The next step, when your students are better at lowering their pulse, is to try this exercise when they are under serious pressure, such as the day of a big test or some on-stage performance in school. If a student can lower his stress level before he leaves for school, he can do it just before the event, and will be more confident and successful.

ACTIVITY 4F Making a Worry Cord

AL Goal: STEAM Learning how art can be used to create an emotional response.

SEL Goal: Self-Management Discovering that a creative design can produce an object of art that can become a powerful ally in the struggle to overcome anxiety.

Any child can learn to use a "worry cord" as a way to quiet his nerves and prepare his mind for effective problem-solving. If your student also believes that the objects on the cord are imbued with special properties (e.g., belonged to a deceased relative), then their efficacy is even greater. The spiritual aspect of this activity is not necessarily religious, but the repetitive nature of moving and holding the objects on the cord creates a serenity that is ultimately relaxing.

Materials Needed: five small objects, which can be attached to a cord (religious medals, small clamshells, tiny toys), and 10 inches of smooth heavy cord. You may want to take students on a nature walk to collect wonderful natural objects that they could attach to it.

Engage: Help each of your students secure the five small objects of their choice with knots on the cord. Let them select the colors and shapes of the objects. Ask students to talk to each other about the little pieces as they place them on the string.

Activate: When students have completed their worry cord, they may use it in any way they like. Feeling the pieces between their fingers as they listen to or sing a favorite song is one option. The mere repetition of moving along the string is calming in itself. Sometimes the use of worry cords in public may draw unwanted attention to your students. You might provide them with an unobtrusive substitute, such as a "magical" flat stone. The stone can be turned in a pocket and rubbed each time a calming phrase is recited.

Reflect: How does this "magic" tool work? Ask your students to discuss this question in small groups. Is its effectiveness mostly:

- Psychological?
- Social?
- Physical?
- Spiritual?

Why do you think so?

Notes

1 Neves, personal communication.
2 Datta, 2016, p. 1.
3 Datta, 2016, p. 1.
4 Henning et al., 2014.
5 Selye, 1956.

5

Be in Control

Self-control is the chief element in self-respect, and self-respect is the chief element in courage.

—Thucydides

I will be calm. I will be mistress of myself.

—Jane Austen

Self-control is getting yourself to do or not do what you want to do or not do, when that is difficult. We add the last phrase because you don't need self-control to get yourself to eat ice cream (assuming you like it). And you don't need self-regulation to get yourself to avoid liver (assuming you don't like it).

Students who are good at self-management learn better than their peers. For example, they:

- Seek out advice[1] and information.[2]
- Commonly seat themselves toward the front of the classroom.[3]
- Seek out additional resources.[4]
- Voluntarily offer answers to questions.[5]
- Manipulate their learning environments to meet their needs.[6]
- Last but not least, perform better on academic tests and measures of student performance and achievement.[7]

These advantages make teaching control one of the highest priorities of SEL.

One stereotype has it that gifted people such as Einstein often lack self-control. Our research[8] and that of others[9] has found this to be false: Most highly talented people are also exemplary in their ability to control their emotions and behavior.[10]

Actually, there are four types of self-control. Shapiro[11] developed a model of self-control that compares four possible actions: positive and negative asserting and yielding.

	Asserting	Yielding
Positive	Active control = positive asserting (dieting)	Passive control = positive yielding (having needed surgery)
Negative	Over-control = negative asserting (anorexia)	Too little control = negative yielding (unable to have needed surgery)

Figure 5.1 Shapiro's Model of Self-Control

Let's consider an activity that demonstrates some differences between these four types of self-control.

ACTIVITY 5A Letting Her Be in Charge

AL Goal: STEAM Define a simple design problem reflecting a need or a want that includes specified criteria for success and constraints on materials, time, or cost.

SEL Goal: Relationship Skills Successfully give over control of the decision-making process to someone else.

Materials Needed: paper and pencil; **Reproducible 5A1: Crossing the Poisonous Peanut Butter Pit**

REPRODUCIBLE 5A1

Crossing the Poisonous Peanut Butter Pit

Your job is to cross over the Poisonous Peanut Butter Pit, which is six feet in diameter (see drawing below). It is so large that you cannot jump over it. To help you, you are given two five-foot boards (that cannot be attached to each other by, for example, nails or screws). First group to solve the problem is the winner, so whisper your ideas to each person in your group. Be sure to "follow your leader."

58 ◆ Self-Management

Engage: Start by gathering your students into groups of four, with at least one female in each group. Appoint one of the girls in each group to be the leader. The goal is to experience yielding leadership to another, especially for the boys who think they should be leader. To work well, the group members must yield control to their leader. Now pass out **Reproducible 5A1: Crossing the Poisonous Peanut Butter Pit**.

Activate: If anyone already knows the solution, ask them to please say nothing. Ready, get set, go. After several groups find the right answer, stop work and tell the class to look at the board as you draw the solution:

Figure 5.2 Solution to the Poisonous Peanut Butter Pit Problem

Reflect: When the task is complete, have a discussion about how it felt to follow the leader's directions:

1. Did your leader do a good job? How or how not?
2. How did having a female leader make you feel?
3. Did anyone think they could do a better job than their leader?
4. Was it frustrating to follow directions even when you didn't want to?
5. What are some situations in which yielding control is necessary (examples: being hypnotized, flying on a commercial plane).
    If you like, let them try to make up a new task. Outward Bound offers many exercises for intermediate pupils. Look them up online: outwardbound.org/

ACTIVITY 5B Control: What Works for You?

AL Goal: Literacy Determine the meaning and appropriateness of phrases as they are used to describe the student.

SEL Goal: Self-Management Gain a better understanding of one's own level of self-control.

Materials Needed: paper and pencil; **Reproducible 5B1: Making Tough Choices**

REPRODUCIBLE 5B1

Making Tough Choices

Suppose you are walking along a road on a warm summer day, and your stomach is growling. You are SO THIRSTY and HUNGRY! However, you realize that the nearest place you can get food is almost two miles in either direction. Even if you run, you know that it's going to be a long time before you can satisfy your powerful needs. You can be miserable until you get to some food and drink, or you can use your mind. What should you do?

Engage: Pass out and ask students to read **Reproducible 5B1: Making Tough Choices**.

Activate: Assign students to groups of four and ask them to think of solutions to the problem presented to them.

Reflect: After an appropriate period of time, ask them to write down what they think of the answers to the following questions:

1. What does the term "self-control" really mean?
2. What are some techniques you might use to distract yourself from your powerful needs?
3. How could "mindfulness" (look it up) be helpful to you?
4. How could "creativity" (look it up) be helpful to you?
5. Who among your friends might you want to ask what they do in these circumstances? What is there about them that you think would make them helpful to you?
6. When you are finished with this activity, perhaps you should make a list of the techniques you find useful and memorize it.

ACTIVITY 5C Step-by-Step

AL Goal: STEAM (Art, Psychology) Drawing an image that signifies what it means to be brave in the face of what feels like a threatening situation.

SEL Goal: Self-Management Doing a self-improvement project when that is hard to do.

Materials Needed: paper and pencil; a two-foot piece of hose or tubing; a toy rubber snake; and a real snake in a glass cage, perhaps at the local zoo [optional]; **Reproducible 5C1: Our Friend, the Snake**

REPRODUCIBLE 5C1

Our Friend, the Snake

In this method for dealing with snake phobia (ophiophobia), we recommend going through a series of steps to achieve a reduction in anxious feelings.

Ask your students to think about a snake.

1. Ask one of them to look at a picture of a snake.

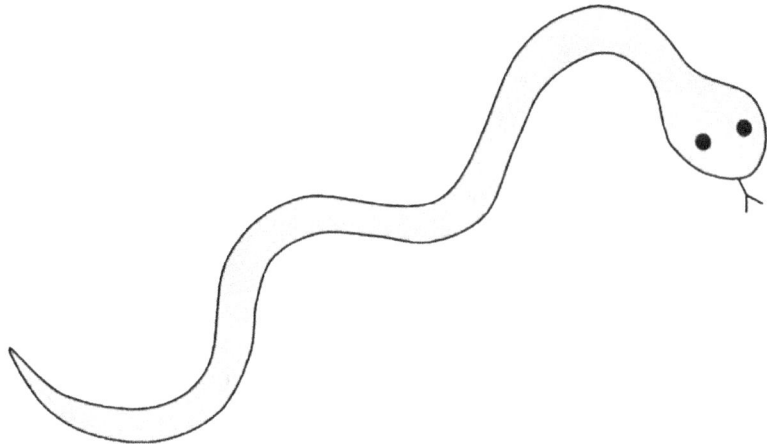

2. Now ask the students to think about the snake while viewing the video at this URL: youtube.com/watch?v=ClwIj3x24Q4

3. Request that he handle a piece of hose while viewing this video again.

4. Then have him handle a rubber snake while thinking about a real one.

5. If possible, take your class on a visit to a zoo and have them look at a snake through the glass cage, without and then with a rubber snake they pass from hand to hand.

6. Ultimately your students may be able to touch and handle a real snake.

© 2018, Taylor & Francis, *Integrating SEL into Your Curriculum*,
John Dacey, Gian Criscitiello, and Maureen Devlin

Engage: Pass out **Reproducible 5C1: Our Friend, the Snake**. Ask students to read it, as well as watch the video, and then discuss as a group whether they think this method might work for someone who has a phobia about snakes.

Activate: Now ask them to think of a situation that is personally either frightening to them, such as being bitten by a dog, or difficult for them, such as stopping biting their nails. When they have identified such a problem (they need not reveal it to their classmates), have them think of a step-by-step strategy for eliminating the problem.

Reflect: In considering their tactics, they should attempt to answer the following questions:

1. The first question they must address is: how big should the steps be? They should be big enough to make serious progress, but not so big as to be extremely difficult.
2. Should there be a reward for each step accomplished, or only when the final goal is reached?
3. If there is to be a reward (or rewards), how powerful should it be? Expert B. F. Skinner recommended that a reward is only acceptable if it motivates desired behavior 95% of the time. That's a pretty powerful reward, or as he called it, a "reinforcement"!

    They will be tempted to give themselves the reward even if they haven't truly achieved the target behavior. It may be better if the reward is given to them by an objective friend.

    Pretty much everyone has more than one thing they don't like about themselves. If they are successful with this procedure, they might like to proceed to another phobia or unwanted characteristic and design another step-by-step procedure to remedy that situation.

ACTIVITY 5D Speed Math?

AL Goal: STEAM (Math) Use multiplication and division to identify combinations of numbers that make up a set of totals.

SEL Goal: Self-Management Maintaining control over one's emotions while mentally racing to be the winner in a class contest.

Materials Needed: pencil; **Reproducible 5D1: Speed Math Exercise; Reproducible 5D2: Speed Math Exercise (Sample Answers—Multiplication); Reproducible 5D3: Speed Math Exercise (Sample Answers—Division)**

REPRODUCIBLE 5D1

Speed Math Exercise

Numbers that may be used only once in each solution:

   2 **3** **4** **5** **6**

+-x*	+-x*	+-x*	+-x*	=	__1__
+-x*	+-x*	+-x*	+-x*	=	__2__
+-x*	+-x*	+-x*	+-x*	=	__3__
+-x*	+-x*	+-x*	+-x*	=	__4__
+-x*	+-x*	+-x*	+-x*	=	__5__
+-x*	+-x*	+-x*	+-x*	=	__6__
+-x*	+-x*	+-x*	+-x*	=	__7__
+-x*	+-x*	+-x*	+-x*	=	__8__
+-x*	+-x*	+-x*	+-x*	=	__9__
+-x*	+-x*	+-x*	+-x*	=	__10__
+-x*	+-x*	+-x*	+-x*	=	__11__
+-x*	+-x*	+-x*	+-x*	=	__12__
+-x*	+-x*	+-x*	+-x*	=	__13__
+-x*	+-x*	+-x*	+-x*	=	__14__
+-x*	+-x*	+-x*	+-x*	=	__15__
+-x*	+-x*	+-x*	+-x*	=	__16__
+-x*	+-x*	+-x*	+-x*	=	__17__
+-x*	+-x*	+-x*	+-x*	=	__18__
+-x*	+-x*	+-x*	+-x*	=	__19__
+-x*	+-x*	+-x*	+-x*	=	__20__

© 2018, Taylor & Francis, *Integrating SEL into Your Curriculum*, John Dacey, Gian Criscitiello, and Maureen Devlin

REPRODUCIBLE 5D2

Speed Math Exercise (Sample Answers—Multiplication)

Multiplication

1 = 3 x 2 − 5
2 = 3 x 2 − 4
3 = 4 x 2 − 5
4 = 2 x 5 − 6
5 = 2 x 4 − 3
6 = 3 x 4 − 6
7 = 2 x 5 − 3
8 = 2 x 4
9 = 3 x 5 − 6
10 = 2 x 5
11 = 3 x 5 − 4
12 = 2 x 6
13 = 3 x 5 − 2
14 = 3 x 4 + 2
15 = 3 x 5
16 = 6 x 3 − 2
17 = 4 x 5 − 3
18 = 3 x 6
19 = 4 x 6 − 5
20 = 4 x 5; 3 x 6 + 2; 3 x 6 + 4 − 2

© 2018, Taylor & Francis, *Integrating SEL into Your Curriculum*, John Dacey, Gian Criscitiello, and Maureen Devlin

REPRODUCIBLE 5D3

Speed Math Exercise (Sample Answers—Division)

Division

1 = 6 / 2 + 3 − 5
2 = 4 / 2
3 = 6 / 2
4 = 6 / 3 + 2
5 = 4 / 2 + 3
6 = 6 / 3 + 4
7 = 6 / 3 + 5
8 = 6 / 2 + 5
9 = 6 / 2 x 3
10 = 6 / 3 x 5
11 = 6 / 2 x 5 − 4
12 = 6 / 2 x 5 − 3
13 = 4 / 2 x 5 + 3
14 = 6 / 2 x 4 + 5 − 3
15 = 6 / 2 x 5
16 = 4 / 2 x 5 + 6
17 = 6 / 2 x 4 + 5
18 = 6 / 2 x 5 + 3
19 = 6 / 2 x 5 + 4
20 = 6 / 2 x 4 + 5 + 3

© 2018, Taylor & Francis, *Integrating SEL into Your Curriculum*,
John Dacey, Gian Criscitiello, and Maureen Devlin

Engage: Pass out **Reproducible 5D1: Speed Math Exercise**. Explain that the goal of this game is to combine two or more of the numbers 2 through 6 to make up all the numbers from 1 to 20. Your students can use each of the five numbers (2, 3, 4, 5, 6) only once in each combination. They can use addition and/or subtraction in any of their solutions but they *must use multiplication at least once in each solution* in their first try at this activity. For example, 3 × 2 + 4 = 10 would be fine, but 3 + 2 + 5 = 10 would not (no multiplication), nor would 2 × 6 – 2 = 10 (using same number twice). The second time they try it, they must use division at least once in each solution, and no number more than once. For example, 6 / 3 + 5 = 7 is one of the correct answers.

Between each box on every row, they can choose one of the following operations: + – × / (add, subtract, multiply, or divide). They should simply cross out this line, and write the sign they have chosen above their cross-out. For example,

would mean multiply the numbers on either side of the x.

Activate (session 1): First try the multiplication exercise. Ask students to raise a hand when they think they are done, and write down the names of the first five. When all are finished, have them trade papers and check the answers. You could pass out **Reproducible 5D2: Speed Exercise (Sample Answers—Multiplication)**, either as a set of examples before they try, or after, as validation (or not at all). Form groups with one of the winners (not including any with a wrong solution) in each group.

Reflect (session 1): Have students discuss these questions:

1. Did you feel nervous about trying to win?
2. Would you have liked it better if this were a homework assignment? Why?
3. Did you employ any relaxation techniques before starting? Or halfway through when you realized you were becoming tense?

[Note to teacher: If you tried any of the strategies in Chapter 4 of this book, you might remind your students now. If not, you might want to introduce one now.]

Activate (session 2): Pass out a second set of **Reproducible 5D1: Speed Math Exercise**, this time to be used for the division exercise. Ask them to raise a hand when they think they are done, and write down the names of the first five. When all are finished, have them trade papers and check the answers.

Reflect (session 2): You could pass out **Reproducible 5D3: Speed Math Exercise (Sample Answers—Division)**, either as a set of examples before they try, or after, as validation (or not at all). Form groups with one of the winners (not including any with a wrong solution) in each group. Have them discuss these questions:

1. Did you feel less nervous about trying to win this time? Why?
2. Would you have liked it better if this were a homework assignment? Why?
3. Did you employ any relaxation techniques before starting this time? Or halfway through when you realized you were becoming tense?
4. As a result of these exercises, has your attitude toward speed tests (competition with classmates or against the clock) changed in any way? How? Why do you think that is?

As we hope you can see, an important element in self-control is an estimation of the amount of risk a person should take. Unfortunately, we teachers often discourage sensible risk-taking, in part by encouraging the quest for the correct answers at all costs. We may even cause our students to be risk-averse.[12] A good analogy here is contact with germs. Many parents do all in their power to insure their children's cleanliness. However, children who live in sterile environments are *more* vulnerable to infection because they do not build up good immunity to infection. Kids *need* to get dirty sometimes.

And we adults need to let them take reasonable risks in other areas of their lives. How do they learn to do this? *Practice*. Only through trying to keep themselves under control as they investigate how risky things can be, and also how risk can be judged accurately, can your students learn to handle risk.

What determines a child's risk-taking capacity? To a certain degree, genes. Some children seem to clamor for scary experiences such as riding on a roller coaster. They explore and expand, and when trouble occurs, they may be dazed but rarely daunted. Other kids are more cautious by nature. Hesitant to venture into unfamiliar territory, they want to preview the script before taking the part. This is why it is so important to support students through inevitable periods of failure or rejection. Without such periods, they cannot learn to manage their emotions or social interactions.

Withdrawing Support

The goal of all education is to make it unnecessary for us always to be present. That is, we want self-management to become engrained in everyday behavior. Thus we need to think about how and when to fade the support our students need in order to achieve mastery. You will need to be on the lookout for signs that class members have internalized self-regulation. Unfortunately, we cannot be specific in our advice on how to do this because there is so much variation in a child's capacity for it. Age, gender, self-confidence, creativity, sensitivity, intelligence, and maturity are all factors that must be considered. What we can say is that you need to be on the lookout for opportunities to *offer practice, to model the skills, and to reward self-mastery*. Teachers who understand that these are among their most vital goals almost always do a fine job of it.

Notes

1 Clarebout, Horz, Schnotz, and Elen, 2010.
2 De Bruin et al., 2011.
3 Labuhn, Zimmerman, and Hasselhorn, 2010.
4 Clarebout, et al., 2010.
5 Elstad and Turmo, 2010.
6 Kolovelonis, Goudas, and Dermitzaki, 2011.
7 Schunk and Zimmerman, 2007; Zimmerman, 2000.
8 Dacey and Lennon, 1999; Dacey and Conklin, 2013.
9 E.g., Selman, 2003; Torrance, 2000.
10 Dacey and Packer, 1992; Dacey and Lennon, 1999.
11 Shapiro, 1993.
12 Sternberg and Lubart, 1995.

6

Think Independently

Blind belief in authority is the greatest enemy of truth.
—Albert Einstein

Freethinkers are those who are willing to use their minds without prejudice and without fearing to understand things that clash with their own customs, privileges, or beliefs. This state of mind is not common, but it is essential for right thinking . . .
—Leo Tolstoy

The ability to think independently means not being overly influenced by others' opinions. An example would be standing up for a classmate who is taunted for his choice of clothing or afterschool activity. Through taking moderate risks, most adults learn to analyze situations, calculate an appropriate response, and follow our own paths. With practice, children can be taught to trust their own judgments, too.

It is important to recognize the influences that impact your students' judgments. As these students develop self-knowledge and become more comfortable taking moderate risks and trusting their own ideas, they will be better able to evaluate the world around them with integrity. This does not mean paying *no* attention to the judgments of others. Rather, it means learning to become observant and objective about those judgments.

If a child's thinking becomes observant and objective, then he has a better chance of making sound decisions. Many factors contribute to our thinking, and much of the time, we are simply operating on automatic pilot. How well we think and act on the spur of the moment is a lot more susceptible to outside influences than we realize.[1]

Some of these outside influences have a strong impact on our judgments, whether it is how much we like the color of someone's tie, or what box we check off on a standardized text next to a prompt for "race/ethnicity." "Mental contamination"[2] (e.g., marketing campaigns) is often harmless but can be, at times, damaging too. It is important for students to be able to critically and accurately navigate the influences around them. A goal for promoting healthy SEL is to encourage children to know themselves, think independently, *and* appreciate the multiple perspectives that help inform their thinking.

The ability to think is the same as intelligence. For example, psychologist Edward deBono states that "[H]ighly intelligent people are not always good thinkers . . . Intelligence is just a potential. Thinking is the skill with which we use that potential."[3] Most formal instruction in thinking occurs in school. Many educational theorists define independent thinking as a quality of utmost importance if we want to nurture a society that is creative, constructive, and collaborative. In part, the purpose of education is to help people think for themselves.[4] The activities in this chapter will help students to learn to access their intellectual potential and develop the ability to successfully think for themselves.

ACTIVITY 6A Dream Me

AL Goal: Literacy Write/create narratives to develop real or imagined experiences or events.

SEL Goal: Self-Awareness Students use self-examination to determine where they are in life and where they are headed in the future.

Materials Needed: paper/pencils or tech device.

Engage: Explain to students that independent thinkers are aware of their interests and passions, and one way to become an independent thinker is to examine your goals and write a narrative of your "Dream Self," a story that tells where you are going in life and why. Further tell students that the more they know themselves, the better they will be able to think independently and achieve their goals in life.

Activate: Ask students to create a narrative of their future selves with a story, cartoon, graphic novel, video, diorama, or other venue identified by children and approved by the teacher. Provide the statements and questions below as a guide:

- If I could be anything I wanted in the future, I would be a _____ because _____.

- What people, places, and objects do you want in your life and why do you want them?

Reflect: Display student creations online or in the classroom/school. Have students read and look at each other's creations. Then reflect together or individually with discussion and/or in writing using the following questions as a guide:

- In what ways is your future-self composition similar or different than your classmates' creations?
- After looking at your classmates' creations, did you want to change your future self? Why or why not?
- How does thinking about your future self help you to strengthen your independent thinking now?

Independent thinkers strive to achieve their goals and dreams. A first step in this process is to understand what your dreams and aspirations are. Looking to the future on their own and with classmates is one way to strengthen students' independent thinking.

ACTIVITY 6B Where Do You Want to Live?

AL Goal: STEAM/Literacy Use design, dialogue, and description to learn about biomes/habitats and visualize what life might be like in a different geographical location.

SEL Goal: Responsible Decision-Making/Self-Awareness Make decisions with a strategic, critical thinking approach.

Materials Needed: pictures of biomes and/or habitats; drawing and coloring pens, paper, glue or tape, and/or a tech device. Linked on website: National Geographic biome video: www.youtube.com/playlist?list=PLmqecn8eUvFzeWKr3Kc21FGN4xSJs438- (and habitat: http://environment.nationalgeographic.com/environment/habitats/); PBS habitat video: http://mass.pbslearningmedia.org/resource/idptv11.sci.life.eco.d4khab/habitat/

Engage: Describe what a biome and/or habitat is. Provide background information via videos, books, or other resources. Ask students to identify the biome or habitat they live in and describe what their "place" is like?

Activate: Ask students to imagine what it would be like to live in a different biome or habitat. Display pictures of those different places by hanging those pictures up in the room or providing a link to the online documents available on the book's website.

Reflect: Each student chooses one place, reads about it, and then writes about and/or draws/builds an image of what life would be like for him in that new place. He describes how life might be different in the new biome and/or habitat, and discusses if he prefers to live in his current location or if he would prefer the new habitat. Providing students with the opportunity to think critically and examine multiple perspectives and possibilities develops their decision-making skills. Making choices like this helps students to trust their instincts and gain confidence and belief in their own decisions and convictions.

ACTIVITY 6C What Do You Really Think?

AL Goal: Literacy Promote rich oral and written independent thinking, conversation, dialogue, and discussion.

SEL Goal: Relationship Skills Teach students to use the Socratic method to refine and revise their independent thinking in a way that arouses depth and bolsters self-esteem. Further explain that using the Socratic method develops their ability to discuss and debate with one another, and this, in turn, builds their relationship skills.

Materials Needed: paper/pencil, a dry erase board, and/or a tech device to record the flow of ideas at this stage and support later stages; **Reproducible 6C1: Teacher/Student Dialogue**

REPRODUCIBLE 6C1

Teacher/Student Dialogue

Teacher: What is the best time of day to study?

Child: In the morning.

Teacher: What time and why is this a good time?

Child: 6 A.M. I'm the first one up in my house, and my house is quiet. I'm rested.

Teacher: What if the study is difficult, and you need help, but everyone else is asleep?

Child: I do all the parts I know how to do and add a question mark at the side of the parts I don't know how to do. Then when others wake up, I ask for help.

Teacher: What if you oversleep?

Child: I stick to a schedule and go to bed early every night. I set my alarm. I never oversleep.

Engage: Tell students that Socrates lived over 2,500 years ago in Greece. When people speak about him today, it's often because of the way he taught people to think and to ask themselves questions about their thinking. He developed a method for this kind of thinking that is now called the "Socratic method," or "dialogue." When two people speak together, that's a dialogue, and that's exactly what Socrates was encouraging people to do—to question each other to get to the heart of their true beliefs. This Socratic method helps individuals to develop independent thinking skills with confidence, precision, and depth.

Activate: We know that the more students take charge of their own learning, the more successful their learning will be. Taking charge or having ownership of learning relies on independent thinking and good choices. Choose one of the following study prompts to begin a Socratic dialogue with students, or come up with one of your own prompts:

- What is the best time of day to study?
- What are the best tools for learning?
- What helps you to succeed as a student?
- Where do you like to study best?
- How do you inspire yourself to study and learn?

Begin with a simple and straightforward question such as the questions listed above. Use the process of questioning and questioning again so the students will learn to chisel away at their thinking until there is no longer any room for contradiction or questioning. Sometimes this takes a long time, and sometimes this moves more quickly. Here is an example of how this might flow: (Pass out **Reproducible 6C1: Teacher/Student Dialogue**)

Reflect: This type of exchange continues until everyone feels content that it's a natural resting point, or a point when they are ready to move on to something else. The goal is to stimulate students' thinking, to examine ideas from different angles, and to build the ability to converse about topics in productive, positive ways. Next, give students an opportunity to try out the Socratic method with a partner. They can do this orally or by writing/keyboarding a written dialogue. A collaborative online document such as Google docs serves as a good vehicle for this kind of exchange. One student acts as the questioner, similar to the teacher role in the example, and the other responds as the student. Back and forth they take turns until they reach a natural resting point. Then they switch roles and start again. A process like this helps students to think deeply about who they are as students and what supports their individual learning success. This process also develops students' ability to engage in rich dialogue as well as objective listening.

ACTIVITY 6D Curiosity: A Critical Ingredient

AL Goal: Literacy Interpret and explain information presented visually, orally, or quantitatively in charts, graphs, diagrams, time lines, titles, animations, or interactive elements on the Web.

SEL Goal: Self-Management To encourage students to take an active interest in their world to develop independent thinking and their own ideas.

Materials Needed: newspapers and/or magazines such as *Time, National Geographic, Smithsonian, Scholastic News,* or other print/Internet materials that feature current events from a global perspective; scissors; tape or glue; pencil/pen; paper. (See website links for related student newspapers and links)

Engage: Explain to students that independent thinkers are curious, and they often use newspapers, magazines, and the Internet to learn about the world around them. Further tell students that study prompted by curiosity also helps students to manage their time and choices in order to engage in activities that are most interesting to them. Use the think aloud approach to model how you survey information and identify media images, diagrams, graphs, and stories that interest you. As you model your approach, include statements that reference the experiences, interests, passions, questions, future plans, and dreams that prompted you to notice the selected media.

Activate: Pass out age-appropriate newspapers and magazines or provide a list of Internet news links (see Internet news links on website). Encourage students to survey the information, choose up to 10 articles or images that interest them, and create a collage of those articles and images.

Reflect: Ask students to reflect on their collages with the following questions:

- What are the main topics of the articles and images you chose?
- How do these topics relate to your interests, passions, experiences, and questions?
- Do you want to read or study more about any of the topics depicted on your collage? If so, why do you want to study and learn more about those topics and how might you do that in the coming days and weeks?
- How does an activity like this help you to manage your choices, time, and behavior? What impact does that have on your overall ability to live a good life?

Independent thinkers are curious and want to learn about the world around them. They use that knowledge to evaluate themselves and their choices, dreams, and direction. Independent learners establish regular patterns of reading and research to persistently develop their independent thinking, self-management, and resulting activity.

ACTIVITY 6E The Design Process

AL Goal: STEAM Conduct experiments. Plan and carry out fair tests in which variables are controlled and failure points are considered to identify, model, or prototype solutions.

SEL Goal: Relationship Skills Listen to classmates' points of view objectively and share one's own point of view confidently.

Materials Needed: a classroom area to display materials including wrapping materials such as bubble wrap, tissue paper, cardboard, recycled egg containers, and adhesives such as tape, staplers, and string.

Engage: Explain to children the difference between a prediction, an educated guess, and a hypothesis. "A hypothesis is an explanation about something you're noticing, or a problem that you can investigate further. For example, you might notice that every time you throw an egg, it breaks. If I ask you to create a container that will protect an egg from breaking if thrown from a high place, what kind of hypothesis can you create about a safe egg package?" Further explain that "when designers and researchers in any field get together to solve a problem, they rely on both independent thinking and group think; one without the other usually does not lead to the best possible solutions. To work with a design/research team in this way takes strategy, skill, and practice beginning with a focus on your own independent thinking, ideas, and solution."

Activate: Ask the students to consider the following questions:

- What do you know about eggs?
- How should delicate objects be protected?
- What's important about transporting eggs safely from one place to another?
- What materials will you use to create a design for a sturdy egg container?
- How will you design the container, and what will it look like?

Ask students to look at the supplies on the display table and draw a model of a sturdy egg container that uses one or more of those supplies. Tell students to clearly label their drawing so others will understand how the egg container is made and what materials are used. Next, place students

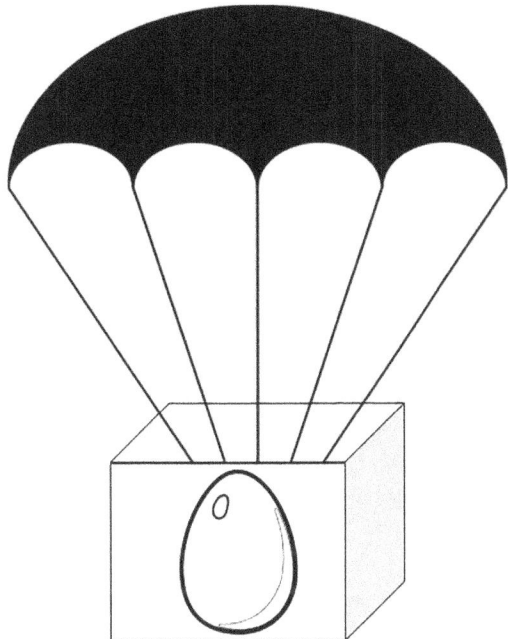

Figure 6.1 The Egg Drop Model

in teams of three or four. Tell students to create an egg container together using the following strategic process:

- Each student presents his model while other teammates listen objectively to the description and write notes that list what they believe to be the pros and cons of the design.
- Display all models within easy view of the group. Together students discuss the designs and then come up with a group design.
- The group creates a prototype and tests it.
- Later the group refines the prototype and completes a design for the egg toss test.

Reflect: In the end, students are asked to reflect individually and as a group using the following questions as a guide:

- Were you able to confidently share your individual design ideas? What helped you to do this successfully and what else would have helped you to do this better?
- Were you able to objectively listen to each other's design ideas? How did this help you to develop your own independent thinking?

- How did each individual's independent thinking contribute to the group's final design?
- Do you think your group design profited from the opportunity for each team member to design his own model first and then share that design with the group? Why or why not?

The success of STEAM projects relies on students' ability to think independently as well as to objectively listen to and assess the thoughts and ideas of others. It's often difficult for students to share their independent thinking with classmates, yet successful learning depends on this. Providing students with a strategic approach to independent thinking and objective listening supports students' confidence and skill in this area. This same approach can be used with almost any STEAM activity, including the marshmallow-spaghetti tower and note-card tower challenges listed on this book's website.

ACTIVITY 6F Culture Flags

AL Goal: STEAM To recognize that our culture and environment influences our behavior, experiences, and ideas.

SEL Goal: Relationship Skills Recognizing that culture influences every aspect of our affiliations.

Materials Needed: banner-sized/shaped colored paper; magazines; drawing/coloring tools; glue

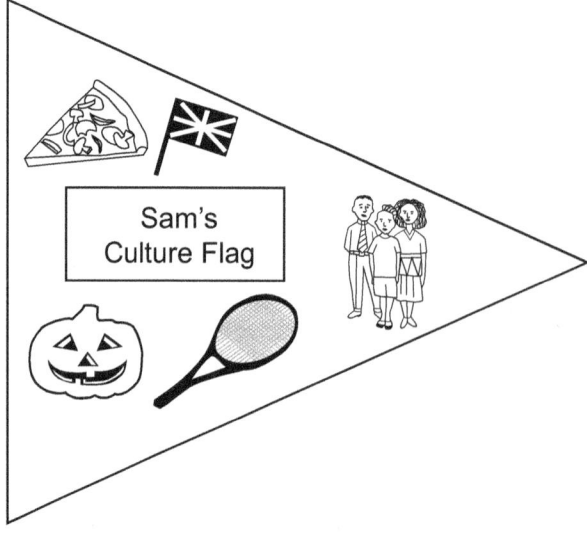

Figure 6.2 Culture Flag

Engage: Explain to students the definition of culture: Culture is the study of the materials, traditions, social groups, beliefs, and arts of groups of people. No two people share exactly the same culture because people belong to many different groups, possibly including their school, religious organizations, clubs, teams, countries of origin/ancestry, race, neighborhood, and more. Tell students that they will make culture flags to depict their unique culture.

Activate: Brainstorm with children images and words that would depict the materials, arts, social groups, traditions, and beliefs that make up their collective culture. Then let students choose a banner color they like and begin to make their own culture flag with pictures and words that depict the everyday life objects, special events, arts, social groups (religious, school, teams, clubs), traditions (holidays, seasonal), and beliefs they have. It's best if the teacher makes up his own flag as an example to follow.

Reflect: Hang up the flags in the classroom for all students to see. Have students examine each other's flags to determine how their personal cultures are similar and different. Discuss that knowing and understanding your unique culture helps you to develop as an independent thinker—the kind of thinker who is aware of his/her own culture and sensitive to the cultures of others too.

Notes

1 Gladwell, 2005.
2 Gladwell, 2005; Greenfield, 2011.
3 deBono, 1993.
4 Gilbert, 2014.

7

Be Resilient

You may write me down in history
With your bitter, twisted lies,
You may tread me in the very dirt
But still, like dust, I'll rise.

—Maya Angelou

Once upon a time, the story line goes, kids were raised in a tough environment. They had to do hard manual chores around the house and they got in fights on the playground. Then they went off to do grueling work in the factory or they learned toughness and grit in the military. But today, helicopter parents protect their children from setbacks and hardship. They supervise every playground conflict, so kids never learn to handle disputes or deal with pain.

There's a lot of truth to the narrative that children in the past were more resilient, but let's not be too nostalgic for the past. A lot of what we take to be the toughness of the past was really just callousness. There was a greater tendency in years gone by to wall off emotions, to put on a thick skin—for some men to be stone-like and uncommunicative and for some women to be brittle, brassy and untouchable.

[So what do we want today?] The people we admire are not hard; they are ardent. They have a fervent commitment to some cause, some ideal or some relationship. That higher yearning enables them to withstand setbacks, pain and betrayal.

—David Brooks

This chapter describes resiliency: the ability to recover from frustration or failure. This is one of the most desirable traits in the SEL pantheon. The critical first step in achieving resiliency is the ability to calm the mind when tempted to panic.

Why do some students handle anxiety so much better than others? While some researchers speculate that resilience is genetic and therefore an innate quality, several studies show that it can be cultivated.[1] Here are the main attributes (sometimes called "protective factors") that distinguish resilient people. They often:

- Perceive bad times only as temporary, and refrain from blaming themselves.
- Do not let hardships define them, and often set goals that inspire them to rise above painful obstacles or grief.
- Recognize their strengths.
- Challenge themselves to be honest.
- Respond actively and creatively to remain positive.
- Possess qualities that elicit positive reactions from those around them.
- Exhibit a high level of self-regulation.
- Reach out to an adult who can offer moral support.
- Have a special interest or talent, such as a knack for working with animals. Their interests absorb them and help to shelter them from negativity.
- Have superior intelligence and problem-solving skills.
- Elicit support, warmth, advice, and comfort from friends.
- Avoid association with delinquent peers.[2]

ACTIVITY 7A Building Your Personal Timeline

AL Goal: Literacy To understand how timelines, a record of events, can facilitate writing about the lives of individuals and societies.

SEL Goal: Self-Awareness Understanding that change to our personalities is inevitable.

Materials Needed: to be used in conjunction with *any* study of a period in which a timeline may be used (e.g., Native American, Medieval Europe, Colonial New England, or one's own personal story/memoir); **Reproducible 7A1: Sample Timeline**; pencil

REPRODUCIBLE 7A1

Sample Timeline

© 2018, Taylor & Francis, *Integrating SEL into Your Curriculum*,
John Dacey, Gian Criscitiello, and Maureen Devlin

Engage: Timelines are frequently used to visually represent periods of history. Here is an example: Distribute **Reproducible 7A1: Sample Timeline**. Discuss with the class what events along the timeline have changed the lives of the people of some particular period. Were the changes good or bad? A timeline, therefore, is a way to keep track of changes in the lives of people.

Activate: Tell the class that they will develop a timeline of changes in their own lives. Pass out the sheet of paper and have them begin with the date they were born on the left side, and then draw a line across the page ending with the present. Have students mark and label big events that have happened to them. These events should be about changes in their lives, for instance, moving from one place to another, the loss of a pet or making a new friend. Next, ask them to write a paragraph about how they were affected by one of the change events.

Reflect: When they are finished, arrange the students into small groups and ask them to read their paragraphs to each other. After the sharing, lead a discussion that focuses on change and how it can affect our lives. Some questions that may help in this discussion:

- What does change mean?
- When do you know things in your life have changed?
- How does change feel when it happens to you?
- Are there different kinds of change, and how may they affect people differently?
- How do people adapt to change?
- Can negative change become positive? How?
- What do you think is the best way to handle change when it happens to you?

ACTIVITY 7B Should I Dare to Do It?

AL Goal: STEAM Better grasp of probability, data collection, display, and analysis.

SEL Goal: Self-Awareness Develop resiliency through understanding one's own capacity to assess risks.

Materials Needed: pencil; **Reproducible 7B1: Scary Stuff?**

REPRODUCIBLE 7B1

Scary Stuff?

Please rate the following activities on a scale of 1 to 4 where 1 means "Low Risk" and 4 means "High Risk."

A. Bungee jumping.

B. Crossing the street when the sign says "don't walk."

C. Roller coaster riding.

D. Reading a poem at an all-school assembly.

E. Helping a stranger who is looking for his lost puppy.

F. Swimming a mile across a river.

G. Putting down a guessed answer on a test.

H. Introducing a friend to a person whose name you're not sure of.

© 2018, Taylor & Francis, *Integrating SEL into Your Curriculum*,
John Dacey, Gian Criscitiello, and Maureen Devlin

Engage: Collecting data from a group of students can help tell us about the group and about ourselves as individuals. This activity begins by assessing risk through thinking about possible outcomes to given situations and the likelihood of those outcomes happening. To get the students started, discuss the meaning of the following terms: "outcome," "possible," "likely," "unlikely," and "impossible." Then talk about what risk means, and the difference between something that is a high-risk activity and a low-risk one.

Activate: Present **Reproducible 7B1: Scary Stuff?**

When the class is finished, collect the ratings and ask a student to make a tally sheet showing how many 1s, 2s, 3s, and 4s each activity received. Show this raw data to the students and have them work with partners or in small groups to come up with a way to best display the data using bar graphs or pie graphs. Share the graphs that each group of students developed.

Reflect: Display the graphs and ask, "What do you notice?" and "What do you wonder?" to begin the discussions. Here are some other questions to stimulate thinking and discussion:

- Which activities got the most "High Risk" ratings? Why?
- Which activities got the most "Low Risk" ratings? Why?
- What are some possible outcomes for these activities?
- Why do you think someone may have rated an obvious High Risk activity as a Low Risk activity?
- Why do you think someone may have rated an obvious Low Risk activity as a High Risk activity?

Explain to pupils that assessing risk happens on a daily basis. Those who take tiny risks or huge risks are less likely to be successful. Successful people are those who know how to determine what a moderate risk is, and then confidently take it, especially if they are recovering from a failure.

ACTIVITY 7C Bring on the Grit

AL Goal: Literacy To gain deeper understanding of literature through character analysis.

SEL Goal: Self-Awareness To understand the importance of persevering through difficult times.

Materials Needed: a selection of literature with which students are familiar that features a character who has struggled to overcome an array of difficulties. Some examples: *Harry Potter*, *I am Malala*, any biography of Dr. M. L. King Jr., or other relevant stories. **Reproducible 7C1: Failure Charts**

REPRODUCIBLE 7C1

Failure Charts

In the past:

Something that I failed at in the beginning.	What did I do to get through it?	Who was there to help me?

In the future:

Something that I may fail at in the beginning.	What could I do to find success in the end?	Who could help me along the way?

© 2018, Taylor & Francis, *Integrating SEL into Your Curriculum*, John Dacey, Gian Criscitiello, and Maureen Devlin

Engage: Make sure that students have read the chosen literature. Lead a discussion about the character and how she struggled through the course of the story.

- What were some of the hardships the character faced?
- How did the character deal with these hardships? Who was there to help?
- How were they helped?
- How do you think the character was able to succeed in the end?

Activate: Students should now describe a time when something used to be difficult for them. This can be as simple as tying their shoes, beginning a musical instrument, swimming, or riding a bike. Pass out **Reproducible 7C1: Failure Charts** and have students fill in the "*In the Past*" part. Have students then think ahead in their lives and identify something that they might, at first, fail at. Fill in the "*In the Future*" part.

Reflect: When they are finished, have students share with partners, small groups, or with the whole class both parts of **Reproducible 7C1: Failure Charts**. After the sharing, lead a discussion that focuses on how students overcame the failure and who may have helped them. Ask:

- What were some difficulties or failures you have had in your life?
- How did you feel when you were faced with these difficulties?
- How did you get through the failure?
- Who helped you to get through it?
- Do you think you could transfer what you did to succeed to other situations where you might fail?
- Who did you reach out to to get help?

ACTIVITY 7D Humor Helps

AL Goal: *Literacy* Writing descriptive paragraphs.

SEL Goal: *Self-Awareness* Learn to find humor in difficult times.

Materials Needed: paper and pencil

Engage: Ask students to tell a funny, personal story or an appropriate joke. Ask the class to look around the room and try to find something funny that others could notice. Explain that we all have stressful experiences in our lives. Sometimes those experiences happen on a regular basis. That's when we need to "Pick ourselves up, dust ourselves off, and start all over again." Trying to find humor during experiences that cause stress can help us handle those hard times.

Activate: Ask students to choose a time when they have experienced stress or anxiety. Have them write a paragraph about that experience. Ask them to then think of something funny that is related to that experience. It could be a joke or anything they feel is funny. Have students share their paragraphs and focus on what humor they found in their experiences.

Reflect: Lead a discussion about the writing and what students found to be funny.

- What did you hear?
- What was funny?
- Have you ever laughed at something you did?
- Was it difficult to find something funny to think of?
- What helped you to think about something humorous?
- Do you think you could find something funny during any situation you are in?
- Do you think you could use humor to alleviate stress the next time something is worrying to you?

Notes

1 Bethell, 2014.
2 Masten, 2014.

Part III
Social Awareness

8

Cooperate and Compete Successfully

A teacher stood at her classroom window on a cold, rainy November afternoon. She could see the football team doing calisthenics. Most of the players were smiling, and all were enthusiastic. "We need that kind of motivation in here," she thought. "What makes playing football so much more valuable to them?"

Immediately the answer came to her:

- There is great joy in working together as a team for a common goal.
- The common goal is to win in competition against other teams.

Why not in the classroom, she wondered? As you undoubtedly know, this creative concept has not swept the world of education. Why not?[1]

When administrators, coaches, parents, and fans understand competition and are committed to helping children get the most from their competitive experiences, it is viewed almost universally as positive. However, when members of any of these important adult groups, particularly coaches, lose perspective and fail to put the child's welfare first, competition can become a negative experience.[2]

Competition is everywhere. We are constantly being encouraged to compare ourselves to others. In fact, evolution programmed it into our genes.[3] Schools are rated on their test scores, colleges on their graduates' success, teams on their win/loss records. Employees are rewarded with higher salaries and promotions, beauty pageant contestants by winning Miss Whatever (or the always-dreaded Miss Congeniality).

Clearly, there are situations in which competition provides the best motivation. However, educational research suggests that students do better when they work cooperatively.[4] Far from "survival of the fittest," the human story could be titled "survival of the most connected." This is true for families, neighborhoods, and nations.[5] And SEL can help. Here are strategies for fostering each of them.

ACTIVITY 8A Alphabet Actors

AL Goal: Literacy Learn to use cooperative skills to achieve an objective, and write a description of what those skills are.

SEL Goal: Social Awareness Develop core skills of communication and perspective-taking, and sometimes conflict resolution as well.

Materials Needed: none

Engage: Tell students they are going to work together in small groups, using their bodies to form letters.

Activate: Divide them into groups of three. Then call out a letter, and tell the groups to form that letter. The groups can decide if they want to build the letters standing or laying on the ground. The first group to form that letter recognizably wins that round.

Reflect: Now ask the groups to work together to answer the following questions:

- If your group was the first to form one of the letters, why do you think you were successful?
- When you lost, why did you lose? If you are never first, what was your group's problem?
- Which was most important in being successful, cooperation or competition?
- What can you tell me about your group's communication skills?
- Would you like to try a new challenge, such as getting a group of your friends to scale a high wall?

ACTIVITY 8B Goldilocks Games

AL Goal: STEAM (Psychology) Learn to use criteria to rate one's performance and apply those judgments in real situations.

SEL Goal: Self-Awareness/Responsible Decision-Making Learn to use criteria to rate one's self and to apply those judgments in real situations.

Materials Needed: pencils; **Reproducible 8B1: Data Recording Sheet**

REPRODUCIBLE 8B1

Data Recording Sheet

Activity	Above Average	Average	Below Average	Agree/Disagree
Writing				
Math				
Running speed				
Strength				
Good manners				
Reliability				
Honesty				

© 2018, Taylor & Francis, *Integrating SEL into Your Curriculum*,
John Dacey, Gian Criscitiello, and Maureen Devlin

Engage: Pass out **Reproducible 8B1: Data Recording Sheet.** Ask your students to think about the activities on this form and how well they think they are able to practice them. (On the blank rows, add any other abilities you would like to rate.)

Activate: Tell your students that for each of the activities of this questionnaire, they should check the box next to it that best describes how capable they are in that trait: below average, average, above average. Then pair them up in twos according to your judgment of how well the students know each other. They should use a second copy of the form to rate how skilled they think their partner is in each of these activities.

Reflect: Now ask them to:

- Make note of which ratings they agree on, and on which they disagree.
- Ask them what's the best way for them to figure out which one of them was right?
- What's the best way to use this information when they are deciding which competitions to enter?

ACTIVITY 8C Good Sport

AL Goal: Literacy Learn to express oneself well in a complex social situation.

SEL Goal: Responsible Decision-Making Learning to gain control over contradictory feelings when competing.

Materials Needed: paper and pencil; **Reproducible 8C1: Questions** (A set of 10 questions that can easily be answered by those in the grade you are teaching)

REPRODUCIBLE 8C1

Questions

1. "What is the date today?"
2. "How many kids are in your group?"
3. "What is your teacher's last name?"
4. "What is the principal's last name?"
5. "What is the name of our school?"
6. "What part of our country is the state in?"
7. "How much are 2+3+6?"
8. "What is the capital our state?"
9. "About how old is the average student in this class?"
10. "In what section of the building is our classroom situated?"

Engage: Ask your students if they have ever met anyone who is just naturally a good sport? These would be individuals who never get mad at other people or at themselves when they lose? Tell them you never have either! This is probably because of the Dunning-Kruger effect,[6] which is "the tendency of unskilled individuals to believe their abilities are better than they really are."

Activate: Divide the class into two equal groups with one group sitting on the left of the room and one group sitting to your right. Explain the rules of the game to the students. You will question them on the left first. If they get the correct answer, they get one point. If they don't, you will ask the same question to the students on the right, and if they get the correct answer, they will get two points. Ready?

Using **Reproducible 8C1: Questions** as a guide, begin asking your questions, and keep a record of the score of the group on the left. You can be confident that pretty soon, the group on the right will start to complain: "Hey, that's not fair!" "The questions you're giving them are too easy!" "They're cheating, we don't have a chance!" "Why should you treat them special? There is nothing special about them!"

Reflect: Now say to the children on the right, "Okay, you are correct, this game was not fair. You never had a chance to score points because the questions were too easy, and the other group got all of them right. I can understand why you got upset. However, suppose you were trying to be a good sport about it. What would you have said instead?"

The children will probably say things like, "Congratulations, you won!" or "You guys did a nice job!" Now ask the group who won the contest:

- "How did it feel when someone accused you of being cheaters?"
- "Was it better when they said, 'Nice job,' even though you knew you only won because the questions were so easy?"

Now some questions for the whole class:

- "How can we decide what is fair and what is unfair?"
- "Can you think of any time when you have been a good sport?"
- "What helps you to be more cooperative and less competitive?"

ACTIVITY 8D Look, Mom, No Hands!

AL Goal: STEAM Understanding the properties of certain materials.

SEL Goal: Relationship Skills Develop interpersonal cooperation skills.

Materials Needed: six empty cans (soda, soup, etc.—have some students bring them in). One string 10 inches long (could also be a strong rubber band), with four "handles" attached to it. The handles are four pieces of string six inches long. See **Reproducible 8D1: Cooperative Can Mover**; **Reproducible 8D2: Empty Cans, Loose and Stacked**

You needn't show the photo to students unless you'd like them to construct their own. You could make one for each team of five in your class, or not.

REPRODUCIBLE 8D1

Cooperative Can Mover

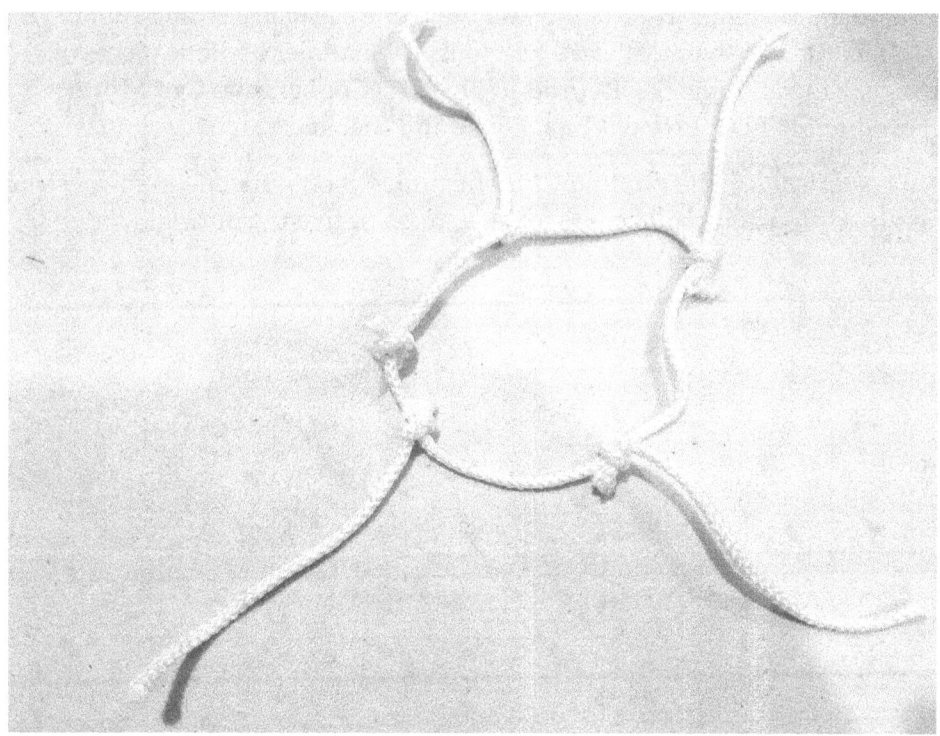

© 2018, Taylor & Francis, *Integrating SEL into Your Curriculum*,
John Dacey, Gian Criscitiello, and Maureen Devlin

REPRODUCIBLE 8D2

Empty Cans, Loose and Stacked

© 2018, Taylor & Francis, *Integrating SEL into Your Curriculum*,
John Dacey, Gian Criscitiello, and Maureen Devlin

Engage: Tell students that their goal is to create a tower with their six empty cans—three on the bottom row, two on the second and one on the top (see **Reproducible 8D2: Empty Cans, Loose and Stacked**). To make the tower, they need to work together using ONLY the string tool. They need to work together to pick up and place one can at a time without talking. Tell them they must coordinate their work silently.

Activate: They should decide which four of the five students will form the can-moving team. The fifth student will be the Recorder and will take notes on the process the others employ. Each member of the team is to pull on one of the strings, until the circular string is stretched into a square large enough to fit over a can. (Note: If a can turns over or rolls off the table, participants can pick it up and place it back on the table. Other than that, no touching!) If they succeed quickly, they can create variations: add more cans, turn the top can upside down, set a time limit, etc.

Reflect: When each team of five students have had a try, ask them to gather and discuss their results. Have the Recorders report on what kinds of problems the teams encountered. Use the following questions:

- What was fun?
- What was frustrating?
- What skills did they need in order to succeed? (Examples include non-verbal communication, coordination, patience, willingness to follow a leader.)
- How did they manage to communicate so they could work together?
- How do these skills help people get along or succeed in life? In our family? Our classroom or school?

Notes

1 Coleman, 1969.
2 Burton and Raedeke, 2014.
3 Das, 2013.
4 Cohen, 2011; Slavin, 2013; Johnson, Johnson, and Stamme, 2000.
5 Rifkin, 2009.
6 Wikipedia, 2014.

9

Neither Be a Bully nor Be Bullied

I would rather be a little nobody, then to be an evil somebody.
—Abraham Lincoln

Empathy is about finding echoes of another person in yourself.
—Mohsin Hamid

Teachers must constantly be alert to bullying and be proactive in giving students strategies to recognize and deal with it. Moms Fight Back, an anti-bullying organization reports that

> 74% of 8- to 11-year-olds say teasing and bullying happen at their school, and 15% of high school students report experiencing cyberbullying in the past year. Victims of bullying, the bullies themselves, and even those children who simply witness bullying will struggle in school and sometimes stop attending out of fear, experience low self-esteem, live in a constant state of stress response, become depressed and often turn to violent behavior.[1]

The American Academy of Child and Adolescent Psychiatry states that "close to half of all children will experience school bullying at some point while they are at primary or secondary school."[2] Many others, obviously, will do the bullying.

Many state and local governments have stepped in to create laws around bullying. Although legislation is absolutely critical to enforce policies that will affect children, it's sometimes difficult to identify the players in the bullying cycle. The terms "bully," "victim," and "bystander" are commonly used to describe what takes place. Researchers note that many bullies have been victims of bullying themselves and, therefore, continue a destructive cycle.

Schools and other organizations have developed creative ways to break the cycle of bullying and to foster a more positive culture where bullying is incompatible with school norms.

An insightful statement from a high school student, written in a recent *Huffington Post Teen* online article, is worth sharing here:

> Up until now, our society has been trying to reform bullies while treating victims as martyrs. By focusing on bullies, we have actually given them more power. Instead, we need to shift our focus away from bullying behaviors and concentrate on building the inner strength of all students.[3]

Teamwork, conflict resolution, trust-building, service learning, group identity encouragement, and cooperation and competition are but a few of the complex strategies now being attempted. Successful anti-bullying programs typically attempt to build greater capacity for empathy, which has a direct link to bullying.[4] As discussed in Chapter 3, mindfulness practices (e.g., meditation, centering) build values that are more empathetic and help encourage connectedness and perspective-taking, as well as improve concentration.[5] Similarly, increasing independent thinking, as described in Chapter 6, prepares students to both stand up to bullies and resist the temptation to bully others.

When children are in groups, subtler forms of mistreatment (e.g., shunning) can be as devastating. These understated forms of bullying often tend to occur in smaller schools or in classrooms with fewer children. The activities below prevent bullying by helping students to develop greater empathy, respect for one another, conflict resolution, and healthy ways to work together.

ACTIVITY 9A Trust Walk

AL Goal: STEAM Teach students that animals receive different types of information through their senses, process the information in their brain, and respond to the information in different ways.

SEL Goal: Self-Awareness Help children experience vulnerability in a safe, controlled environment.

Materials Needed: a blindfold, bandana, or scarf.

Engage: Remind students that people are animals, and as animals we use our senses to navigate the world around us. Have students make a list of how humans and other animals may use their senses. Tell them that when one sense is limited or not available, animals typically use and/or strengthen another sense to use in its place. In this activity, they will experience their environment without their sense of sight, the sense they rely on the most. Explain that this will make them vulnerable and that vulnerability will push them to rely more on their other senses as well as the help of a classmate.

Activate: Invite students to pair up. Ask them to decide who will be the first with his eyes closed, and who will be the guide. Say, "We're going to take a walk together. On this walk, one person will have his eyes covered, and one person will be the guide. It is the guide's job to make sure that the person with his eyes blinded is safe. This means making sure that no one bumps into anything, trips over anything, falls, or stubs toes. When you are the guide, you should make the walk as interesting as possible for your partner—you may go up or down stairs, and enter rooms with different sounds or smells. As you're walking, touch different objects or feel different textures on the walls or floors. Take this "trust walk" without anyone speaking. Try to be silent the entire time. Use your imagination only. When I tell you, you will stop wherever you are and switch roles—the guides will put on the blindfolds and those who were blindfolded will now be the guides."

Reflect: When the children have completed their turns as guides and trusting, blindfolded partner, you may discuss some or all of the following questions:

- How did it feel to have your eyes closed and to rely on your partner?
- Did you feel more comfortable blindfolded or as the guide?
- Did you enjoy the trust walk? What did you like most about it?
- What would you change next time?
- Has doing this activity changed you for the better? For example, do you feel more trusting of each other?

ACTIVITY 9B The Conflict Within

AL Goal: ELA All good stories involve a series of events, the plot that involves a problem. Learn how the problem is typically related to a number of choices or decisions a character in the story makes.

SEL Goal: Self-Awareness and Responsible Decision-Making Help students recognize internal conflicts they may be experiencing, and to notice how these conflicts affect them and others.

Materials Needed: conflicts sheets; pencils, crayons, colored pencils for drawing

Engage: Ask students to think about the story of their life. What are some choices they have made recently—today, yesterday, this week, or even this month—and how did these decisions arise from their story? Choices are sometimes complicated, and sometimes they are quite simple. They choose what flavor yogurt to eat for lunch or what television show to watch. Maybe they chose which friend to invite to come over or which classmates to invite to a birthday party.

Sometimes when we make a decision, we feel conflicted about it—we aren't sure if it's right. Maybe there is no right or wrong answer at all! We sometimes find ourselves thinking about whether a choice that we make is in sync with our values, about how we think we are supposed to act.

Activate: Ask your pupils to write down some difficult choices they had to make recently. Which decisions do they feel good about and which ones do they wish they could do over? Did the decisions result in conflict? If so, were they able to resolve those conflicts?

Reflect: Small group discussions:

- In what ways do the choices they have made affect their own life and the lives of others?
- How might they make choices in ways that are more positive?
- When thinking about the books they've read, how have a character's choices made a difference to those around them?
- Can they name a specific example of a choice that a friend has made that either positively or negatively affected them?

ACTIVITY 9C On a Deserted Island I Would Bring . . .

AL Goal: ELA Distinguish their own point of view from that of others.

SEL Goal: Social Awareness and Responsible Decision-Making To help children recognize different strengths in others and how they might better appreciate those strengths.

Materials Needed: index cards or small pieces of paper to write on; pencils

Engage: Explain to students that we are all a mix of strengths and challenges, and that understanding those traits will help us to make good decisions about our pursuits and interests. Ask students to form small groups and make a list together of strengths and challenges they might have. Explain further how point of view and context affect whether we see a trait as positive or negative. A perceived strength on one point of view may be considered a challenge by another, or in a different situation.

Activate: Tell students that they're going to pretend that they are heading to a deserted island for a short stay. Ask students to consider what kind of person would be most helpful to travel with. Then ask them to describe the person they would want to travel with by listing advantageous traits on an index card/piece of paper. For example, a student might say, "I want someone who knows how to cook" or she might say, "I would want someone funny to make me laugh while we're there." Ask students to share their answers with each other. Then say to students, "What were some of the common traits you wrote on your index cards? What characteristics were listed the most? The least?"

Reflect: Ask students to highlight traits that would be helpful on the deserted island, but seen as challenges or not helpful at the playground or at a birthday party. Then say that we have to recognize that our own strengths and challenges and those of others may be helpful and valued in some circumstances, but not in others. Mention that sometimes people quickly judge each other and even worse, bully others. It's important to consider strengths and challenges with a wider view of respect and appreciation. Ask students if they have ever experienced someone judging, teasing, or bullying someone else because of their perception of that person's strength or challenge.

ACTIVITY 9D Tower of Cards

AL Goal: STEAM Plan and carry out an investigation to answer a question or test a solution.

SEL Goal: Social Awareness/Relationship Skills Help children work together to create and complete a collaborative project, which requires listening to and acknowledging others' ideas.

Materials Needed: five sets of 30 index cards

Engage: Acknowledge that a lot of STEAM work requires teamwork. Note that teamwork isn't always easy and requires people to share ideas, listen to one another, create, and compromise.

Activate: Say to students that they're going to work in five small groups for this activity, and that they've got a package of notecards they can use to create a tower. The rules are that each group member gets a chance to participate in the creation, and each teammate helps to decide what that creation will be. Give the players 10 to 15 minutes to work with the notecards. When they are finished, invite them to examine the creations that others came up with.

Reflect: Encourage students to share their ideas and processes with the other children in the class. Some questions for discussion are:

- How did you decide to create your final product?
- What problems did you have coming up with an idea for your creation? Did you have any problems working together to make it?
- How did you negotiate about how to work together?
- What would you do differently next time?

ACTIVITY 9E Reflect, Reflector, Reflect

AL Goal: STEAM Focus on reflection symmetry. The line of symmetry is the mirror line.

SEL Goal: Social Awareness and Responsible Decision-Making Help students recognize that their own impulses and reactions are different from those of someone else.

Materials Needed: paper and pencil; **Reproducible 9E1: Picture That Demonstrates Reflection Symmetry**

REPRODUCIBLE 9E1

Picture That Demonstrates Reflection Symmetry

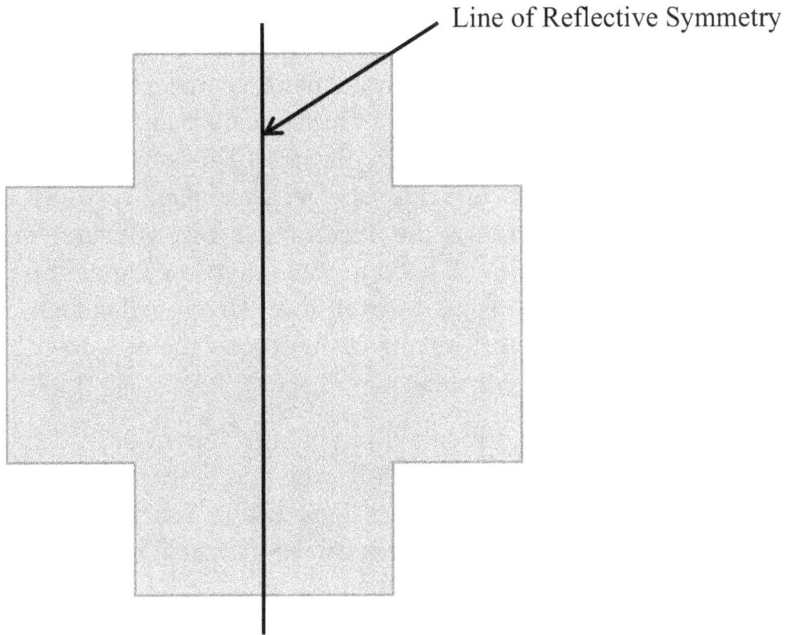

© 2018, Taylor & Francis, *Integrating SEL into Your Curriculum*,
John Dacey, Gian Criscitiello, and Maureen Devlin

Engage: Pass out **Reproducible 9E1: Picture That Demonstrates Reflection Symmetry**. Introduce students to reflection symmetry. Demonstrate reflection symmetry, then tell students that the line of symmetry is considered the "mirror line."

Activate: After that, stand in front of the classroom facing the students. Say to students, "Let's begin the mirror activity. Picture a mirror you have seen somewhere before. What do you see? A mirror shows us our reflection—it shows us what we look like, and any movement we make is copied in the mirror reflection. Face me. Now copy my movements as if you were looking in a mirror. Now we'll do the same with partners. Those of you who are the movers will start to make movements, especially facial expressions, when I signal you. Those of you who are the mirrors will copy your movers' every action as well as you can. You will need to stare at your partner and notice his or her movements, big and small—even tiny! Then we'll switch, and the movers will be the mirrors. The mirrors will copy the movers' actions." (Allow two to three minutes for this.)

Reflect: Ask students what is difficult about being a mover or leader, and what is easy? About being a mirror or follower, and what is easy? In what real or imagined situations could mirroring be used? Are there ways that mirroring the way someone else behaves can be a form of bullying?

Notes

1 Momsfightback.org, 2017, p. 1.
2 AACAP, 2011, p. 1.
3 Baird, 2014.
4 van Noorden, et al., 2016.
5 Flannick, 2014.

Part IV
Relationship Skills

10

Build Successful Friendships

> Compassion is a marvel of human nature, a precious inner resource, and the foundation of our well-being and the harmony of our societies. If, therefore, we seek happiness for ourselves, we should practice compassion; and if we seek happiness for others, we should also practice compassion!
> —H. H., The Dalai Lama

> My best friend is the one who brings out the best in me.
> —Henry Ford

There is something deeply elementary about the desire to be connected to others, and to feel that others wish to connect with us.[1] This mutually reciprocal linking is known by different names, but for our purposes, we will focus on friendships. Our need for attachment has contributed to the rise in social media usage among children and teens, and in the age of the "selfie," children thinking about others as much as themselves seems strange.

Teaching and strengthening the qualities and attributes of friendship is both possible and positive. Research shows that when we think about other people, our minds actually expand.[2] There are portions of our brain that respond when we think kind, compassionate thoughts, and over time—like any exercise—we can strengthen these parts of our brain and contribute to a happier, healthier society at the same time.

Often, when people reflect on their own capacity to behave in a compassionate manner, they face dilemmas. One is that empathy is rarely taught explicitly at home or at school, because it's often "considered intuitive and therefore difficult to teach, or a 'soft' emotional skill."[3] So by explicitly teaching, modeling, and providing opportunities to practice empathy, we teach students to be empathetic by stepping into each other's experiences.

In his brilliant book, *Childhood and Society*, Erikson speaks of "validation," which works in two steps. First we reveal, usually in the form of a confession, something about ourselves to someone in whom we have placed our trust—a friend. This is always a risky proposition, because the friend could easily invalidate our sense of identity by expressing their disgust. Suppose, for example, a student confesses to a friend that he never watches television. If that friend responds by saying, "You never watch TV? That's weird!," the integration of the confessor's psyche is likely to fracture. Now suppose on the other hand, that friend says, "Yeah, I don't spend my time watching TV either." Then the friend goes on to describe the specifics of his own experience, and by this admission, makes himself vulnerable. This friend's approval, followed by his trustful description of his own self-doubting action, is what Erikson means by validation. Elements such as validation, compassion, and empathy, coupled with kindness and respect for the challenges of others, are the foundation of good friendships.[4]

ACTIVITY 10A Detail Detective

AL Goal: Literacy Notice details and understand how noticing details contribute to the comprehension of the overall theme and meaning of an event, story, or text.

SEL Goal: Relationship Skills To encourage your students to pay attention to and remember specific details related to objects and events.

Materials Needed: a cookie sheet or tray; 10 to 15 miscellaneous items that are familiar to students such as food, toys, utensils, tools

Engage: Get a cookie sheet or other serving tray, and place about a dozen different items on it. Position the tray in open view while students are busy with other matters. Later in the day, explain to students that good readers, like good detectives, notice details.

Activate: Remove the tray, give your students a piece of paper and ask them to write the numbers 1 through 12 (or however many items are on the tray) on the paper. Ask students to write down as many items on the tray as they are able to recall. Allow them to take as much time as they need to come up with their answers.

Build Successful Friendships ◆ 115

Figure 10.1 Object Tray

Reflect: Have students pass their answer sheet to the person on the left, who will score it. Show the students the tray and see how many items they were able to remember. Explain to children that just because something is in plain sight doesn't mean that they will notice it. Ask if there have been other times when they didn't notice specific details, times such as while reading a book, during a family or school event, or perhaps for a team assignment or assessment. Have students relay stories about how not noticing the details either negatively or positively impacted relationships in those situations. For example, if a student is so anxious to tell his friends about a special event, he doesn't make the time to greet his friends and notice their current mood or affect, it may turn out that the friend doesn't listen to him.

On the other hand, if the boy had stopped and asked his friends first, "What's new?" and listened to their tales and responses, he may find that they react to his story better. Finally, ask students how they plan to pay better attention to the details related to their friends and family members when they work together, and let them describe how those actions will serve to heighten their relationship skills and happiness.

ACTIVITY 10B I Spy What You Need

AL Goal: STEAM/Literacy Observe carefully and write routinely over extended time frames for a range of discipline-specific tasks, purposes, and audiences.

SE Goal: Self-Management Encourage children to be more aware of the needs of others.

Materials Needed: a clipboard and paper, notebook, journal, or tech device; benches or seats on the playground, in the classroom, or at school where students are able to sit and watch people as they go about their activities.

Engage: Explain to students that we may lead and manage our positive behavior and actions by taking the time to observe the people around us, discover what they need, and then acting to fulfill those needs.

Activate: Tell students that they are going to engage in an activity that writers often employ to notice people's actions and needs. Explain that they are going to sit somewhere around the school for 10 minutes to observe and write down what they notice about the people they see. Tell them that while they are watching, they should use those observations as one way to think about what students need and how they might help those students. Disperse students to their observation posts.

Reflect: Regather and ask students if they were surprised by what they noticed. Ask them if they noticed any student needs. Then discuss how they might lead and manage their own behavior in order to be kind and responsive to students' needs. Explain that this kind of observation and thought enables students to work alone and/or together to help one another and make the school a happier and better learning community. Ask how observations like this might help them to also build good friendships and better their writing too.

ACTIVITY 10C Kindness Cups

AL Goal: Literacy Use concrete words, phrases, and sensory details to convey descriptions, experiences, and events precisely.

SEL Goal: Social Awareness Teach children the power that underlies giving someone a genuine compliment or words/acts of encouragement.

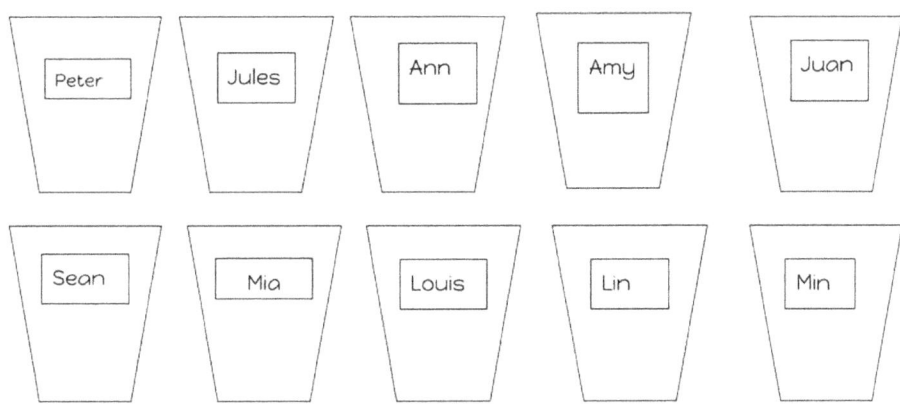

Figure 10.2 Compliment Cup Bulletin Board Model

Materials Needed: index cards, post-it notes, or other pieces of paper; pens/pencils; paper cups with students' names on them hung on a bulletin board or placed on a table; **Reproducible 10C1: Compliment Anchor Chart**.

REPRODUCIBLE 10C1

Compliment Anchor Chart

Characteristics of a good compliment	Words used in a good compliment
E.g., traits mentioned a specific: "Helpful"	E.g., "Alert"

Engage: Make a compliment anchor chart with students (pass out **Reproducible 10C1: Compliment Anchor Chart**). On one side ask students to list words that describe a good compliment, and on the other side list words that students might use when writing a good compliment. Tell students that the best compliments describe genuine efforts, as opposed to labels such as "smart" or "pretty" or "strong." Then refer to and/or read one of the "fill a bucket" books by Carol McCloud.[5] Many school communities have used these books as launch pads for school-wide efforts to be kind to others. These books also help to establish shared vocabulary or language to use when discussing feelings. Another way to frame this is to think about a simple cup. Tape a cup with the student's name on it to the wall.

Activate: Designate specific times during the day when students have the opportunity to fill each other's cups. This could be during a recess, lunch, or any other time that is easy to turn into a routine. Keep a pad of post-it notes or other paper in a designated area next to students' cups, so that anyone who wishes to fill someone's cup is able to do so.

Reflect: As your class begins "filling the cups," and reading the notes, they'll start to notice different strengths and positive inclinations that both they and other students have. Discuss with the students how everyone brings different personality traits, skills, and strengths to their classmates and class events. Ask students to share what they notice about the cups, how the compliments make them feel, and if they have any special related stories to share. Then discuss the role that genuine compliments serve when it comes to building strong friendships.

ACTIVITY 10D Snowflake String

AL Goal: Literacy/STEAM Describe characteristics and variability.

SEL Goal: Self-Awareness Encourage students to think about uniqueness and its role in friendship.

Materials Needed: white pieces of paper, cut into squares approximately 5"× 5" wide; scissors; glue; 7"× 7" squares of colored paper.

Engage: Tell students that snowflakes are both alike and different. Explain that scientists tell us that no two snowflakes are alike, yet they are made of the same molecules. They share the same air space, yet they float on their

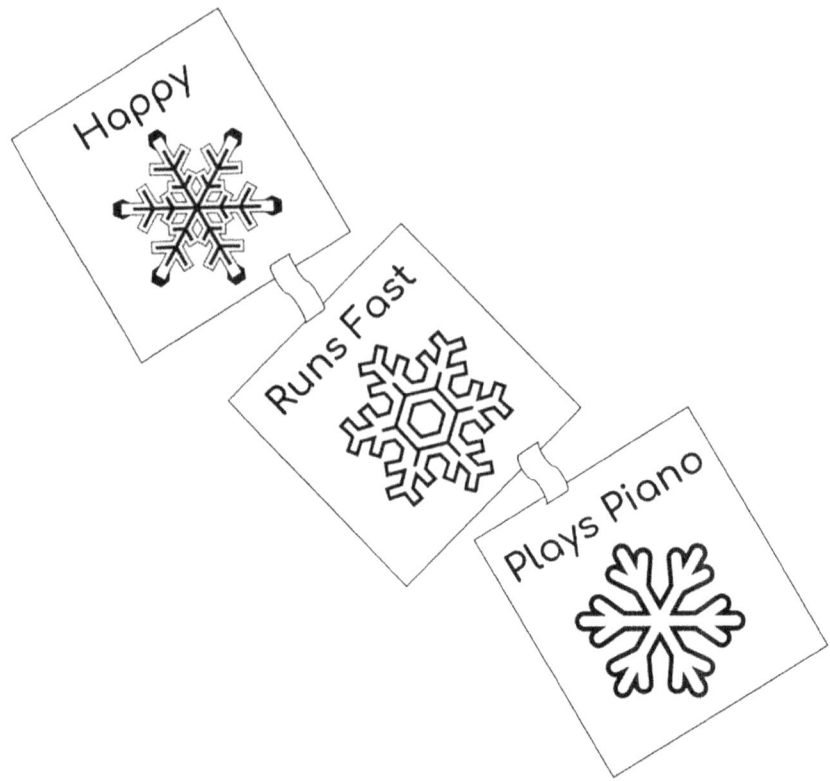

Figure 10.3 Snowflake String Model

own paths as they swirl, drift, collide, and eventually land. Scientists refer to this as variability.

People are a lot like snowflakes. Students should list some ways that people are alike, such as: "We all have skin, hair, eyes, and noses," or "We all are scared sometimes," or "No one is ever perfect." Then ask your students to think about and share some ways that people are different. They might describe different tastes in food, different physical attributes, or different languages and traditions that people have.

Activate: Explain to students that they are to create a "Snowflake String" to represent the unique qualities that represent them or their families. Taking one piece of white paper at a time, children can cut out snowflake shapes. This is accomplished by taking the square piece of paper and folding it in half, and then again into fourths. Each child can experiment with different folding techniques. As your students cut paper snowflakes, ask them to mount the snowflakes on colored paper and then write a unique quality of his own or his family's on the colored paper that frames the snowflake. A child might, for example, write "blue eyes," "shares with others," and "silly" on his snowflakes. Punch holes in each mounted snowflake square and connect the squares with yarn or string. After that, hang up all the beautiful snowflake strings in the classroom to represent the class's variability.

Reflect: After giving students a chance to view each other's snowflake strings, ask them what they noticed about the class's variability. Have them list characteristics that they share and those that vary quite a bit from each other. Ask why they think variability is positive, and when variability can be challenging. Also ask children to discuss when variability is an advantage with regard to friendships and when it can be a disadvantage.

ACTIVITY 10E Treasure Friendship

AL Goal: STEAM/Literacy Make rectangular prism treasure boxes. Explain the meaning of simple similes and metaphors (e.g., as bright as sunshine or he's a real octopus when he wrestles.)

SEL Goal: Social Awareness Teach children about the many different qualities inherent in connections with others, and how those connections help us to develop and treasure friendships.

Materials Needed: small recycled boxes that are rectangular prisms. Students may make these prisms using an enlarged rectangular prism net template or a rectangular prism net that students make on their own. Assorted items for the bags (one of each)—buttons, small rocks, adhesive bandages, cotton balls, stickers, rubber bands, paper clips, and pennies.

Engage STEAM: Introduce students to rectangular prisms. Invite students to make a large rectangular prism on their own or with a template (see link on website). Discuss the attributes of rectangular prisms.

Engage Literacy: Tell students that writers often compare feelings to tangible objects using metaphor and simile. Further, people treasure friends and what friendship brings to their lives. Discuss with students what they think each item in the bag might represent with respect to the treasure that a good friend is. For example, a paper clip could represent how *a friend stays by your side*, a button could remind them that *a good friend makes you feel secure*. Similarly, an adhesive bandage might prompt them to think that *a friend helps us heal*, a rubber band can remind them that *good friends sometimes stretch us or use flexibility to understand and accept us*, and a penny could indicate that *friends are priceless*. There are many variations that your students may think up, and these ideas can open pathways to larger, meaningful conversations that arise.

Activate: Students find recycled prisms from home or make their own. Students may first make their own using the template provided, and later design their own prism templates and prisms.

Reflect: Notice how students have used an array of recycled and handmade prisms. Have students reflect about what is similar in all prisms, and what is different.

Notes

1 Maslow, 1998.
2 Weng et al., 2013.
3 Galinksy, 2010, p. 71.
4 Erikson, 1950.
5 McCloud, 2008.

11

Demonstrate Leadership

It is better to lead from behind and to put others in front, especially when you celebrate victory when nice things occur. You take the front line when there is danger.
—Nelson Mandela

If your actions inspire others to dream more, learn more, do more and become more, you are a leader.
—John Quincy Adams

Effective leaders:

- Want their people to succeed.
- Are not competitive with their team.
- Have an open-door policy (generous with their time).
- Would rather err on the side of grace than be just or strict with policies.
- Are open to new ideas.
- Freely share what they are learning.
- Love to give credit to others even when they could rightly keep it for themselves.
- Care about their team. They know about each team member's goals and dreams, and diligently try to help them fulfill those desires.[1]

All of these qualities of a successful leader are included in the five traits that CASEL identifies as keys to an individual's success in life (see Chapter 1).

These qualities bring success in life not only for those students that are in leadership positions but for all students. If you can imagine your students having all or some of these traits, you would see a classroom where high levels of learning take place. Management consultant Sharon Salzberg posits that success in the workplace is most likely when eight pillars are in place. These pillars are also important for children:

- *Balance:* the ability to differentiate between who you are and what your job is.
- *Concentration:* the ability to focus without being swayed by distraction.
- *Compassion:* being aware of and sympathetic to the humanity of others.
- *Resilience:* the ability to recover from defeat, frustration, or failure.
- *Communication and connection*: understanding that everything you do and say can improve connection or take away from it.
- *Integrity:* integrating your deepest ethical values into all you do.
- *Meaning*: infusing the work you do with relevance for your own personal goals.
- *Open awareness*: the ability to see the big picture and not be held back by self-imposed limitations.[2]

Students' daily lives involve "work," and their "jobs" entail these precise skills. As we grow throughout our lifetimes, the setting may change, but the fundamental skills that help us succeed remain constant. Authentic leadership requires the "bandwidth" and flexibility to help guide a group or organization. One element that has been acknowledged recently in the media is "focus." Famed "emotional intelligence" researcher Daniel Goleman states:

> Leadership itself hinges on effectively capturing and directing the collective attention.
> Leading attention requires these elements: focusing your own attention, then attracting and directing attention from others, and getting and keeping the attention of employees and peers, of customers and clients.[3]

Popular media and characters from literature dating back to the Old Testament portray leaders as being in positions of power. The situations in which these traditional examples of leaders find themselves often include conflict, such as battles and struggles for control over people and possessions. Providing insight into power, Congressman Tim Ryan notes that our perceptions have been influenced over thousands of years by ". . . millennia of warrior traditions . . . focused on training two qualities: wisdom and bravery. Wisdom is defined as the ability to see clearly how things are, not how we want them to be, and then use that information to make the most effective decision in the moment. Bravery . . . is the ability to stay present with any experience, even an extremely difficult one, without needing it to be different."[4] Previously essential? Probably. Essential today? Probably not.

As children develop skills and strategies tied to decision-making—big and small—they learn to make choices about what to ignore and where to focus their attention. This awareness brings with it a responsibility to balance difficult, sometimes contrary elements in order to achieve a desired outcome. Congressman Ryan refers to this as "the ability to be firm and simultaneously to be gentle. This can be challenging, but Martin Luther King, Jr. offered us an example of holding hard and soft together. He pointed out that love without power is ineffectual, and power without love is destructive."[5]

Leadership entails skill in handling and distributing power, and making calculated choices. Also implicit in the notion of leadership is the understanding that others choose to follow the inspiration of a leader.

> Leaders who inspire can articulate shared values that resonate with and motivate the group. These are the leaders people love to work with, who surface the vision that moves everyone. But to speak from the heart, to the heart, a leader must first know her values. That takes self-awareness.[6]

Self-awareness, a vital aspect of leadership, includes having an accurate image of one's strengths and weaknesses. This affords children the opportunity to view themselves as protagonists, directors, and authors of their own stories. Leaders who have a strong awareness of themselves are better able to gain the trust of others. Former president of Wellesley College, Diana Walsh, stated in a lecture, "Trustworthy leadership begins and ends with leaders who can question themselves."[7]

As children become more self-aware, they naturally realize that the self is part of a bigger system. They recognize that we are not alone and that the goal is not independence from family and friends. Rather, it is interdependence with them. This often stirs questions about doing something for one's self in a selfish manner, and doing something for one's self as part of important self-care. Ultimately, children will come to understand that when we "water the seeds of peace in ourselves and those around us, we become alive, and we can help ourselves and others realize peace and compassion."[8] This is among the best goals of leadership.

As Goleman puts it, "[the] most visible leadership abilities build not just on empathy, but also on managing ourselves and sensing how what we do affects others."[9] Demonstrating leadership is one way that children portray their social-emotional competence. The following activities are designed to improve this competence by having children understand power and by expanding their capacity for self-awareness.

ACTIVITY 11A Who's the Boss?

AL Goal: Literacy Reflective writing—have students think and write about an experience.

SEL Goal: Social Awareness Give students an introduction to one form of power.

Materials Needed: paper and pencils; **Reproducible 11A1: Who's the Boss?**, or similar teacher-generated list; **Reproducible 11A2: 3–2–1 Writing Guide**

REPRODUCIBLE 11A1

Who's the Boss?

Command List

- Quack like a duck.
- Sing "Happy Birthday."
- Walk in a circle three times.
- Hop on one foot and clap your hands for 20 seconds.
- Walk up to someone and ask him what time it is.
- Press your thumbs against earlobes and waggle your fingers.
- Sit down, stand up, sit down, stand up, sit down.
- Come here, take this paper, bring it to him, come back, take this paper, bring it to her.

3–2–1 Writing Guide

3 Things—Write down 3 things you enjoyed about this activity

2 Things—Write down 2 things you didn't like

1 Thing—Write down 1 thing you wondered about

Engage: Tell students that some of them will have a chance to be "the boss" for the activity and be able to tell others what to do. Select a student to be "the boss" to begin with.

Activate: Review the list (**Reproducible 11A1: Who's The Boss?**) with "the boss" only and have her choose three things from the list to delegate to other students. When done, choose another "boss" and have her choose three things from the list to delegate to others. Repeat one or two more times. When done, have the students write a 3–2–1 paragraph (**Reproducible 11A2: 3–2–1 Writing Guide**) where they describe 3 things they liked about the activity, 2 things they didn't like, and 1 thing they wondered about.

Reflect: Have students share their 3–2–1 writing and then lead a discussion about the activity. Use these questions to get the discussion going.

- What did you like about being the boss? How did it feel?
- How did it feel to be told what to do?
- How would you feel if you were the boss all the time?
- How would you feel if you were never the leader?
- How can someone be a better boss?
- What power do people usually have over you?
- What power do you usually have over other people?
- What power do you have over yourself?

ACTIVITY 11B Power People . . .

AL Goal: Literacy Paragraph writing.

SEL Goal: Social Awareness Help students recognize qualities that are associated with people in power.

Materials Needed: paper and pencils/pens for writing; pictures of people in power from magazines and newspapers

Engage: Show students pictures of people who represent power from magazines, cartoons, or favorite stories. Ask students who comes to mind when they think about people in "power."

Activate: Have students list as many of the most powerful people they know or know about. These can be people they have met, people they have seen or heard about on television or online, and even fictional characters from stories they've read. Students then choose one of these people to write a paragraph where they describe what that person does with a focus on what they have power over.

Reflect: When students have completed their writing, ask some to share their lists or paragraphs. Use the questions below as a basis for conversation:

- How do you know these people are powerful? What does the word "power" mean?
- Are all of these people really leaders? If so, how do you know, and whom do they lead?
- How do they use their power?
- Do you believe that these people think they are powerful?
- What do these people have in common?
- How are these individuals different?
- Are some people in power better at what they do than others? Why?

ACTIVITY 11C Decisions Have Consequences

AL Goal: Literacy Reading comprehension through plot analysis.

SEL Goal: Responsible Decision-Making To help students recognize that different decisions have different consequences.

Materials Needed: **Reproducible 11C1: Decisions and Consequences;** examples from books that the students are familiar with where characters have made decisions that result in consequences. It could be a class novel or *Choose Your Own Adventure* novels, where the endings are ambiguous, cliff-hangers, or otherwise undetermined.

REPRODUCIBLE 11C1

Decisions and Consequences

Original Decision	Consequence	Alternative Decision	Possible Consequence #1	Possible Consequence #2

© 2018, Taylor & Francis, *Integrating SEL into Your Curriculum*,
John Dacey, Gian Criscitiello, and Maureen Devlin

Engage: Ask students if they've ever noticed that after making a decision, sometimes things work out fine and sometimes there are surprises? No matter how hard we might try to think of all of the risks involved in making a decision, we may forget a detail or two.

Activate: Describe the example from the book you have chosen and ask students to identify the decision that the character has made. Ask them to describe the outcome of the decision. Have students fill in the appropriate boxes in **Reproducible 11C1: Decisions and Consequences**. Ask them to think and record an alternative decision the character could have made and one or more possible consequences to that decision.

Reflect: Have students share their alternative decisions and the possible outcomes that happened as a result. Use the following questions to lead a discussion about how decisions have consequences that we can't think of in the moment.

- Why do you think the author had the character make the choice he/she did in the story?
- How different were your decisions from the characters?
- How many different possible consequences did we think of?
- Can you remember a time when you have made an important decision?
- What were the outcomes of your decision?
- How would things be different if you had decided differently?

ACTIVITY 11D Personal Shield of Pride

AL Goal: STEAM (Art—drawing)

SEL Goal: Self-Awareness Help children recognize their own strengths and connection to others.

Materials Needed: **Reproducible 11D1: Personal Shield**; crayons, markers, colored pencils

REPRODUCIBLE 11D1

Personal Shield

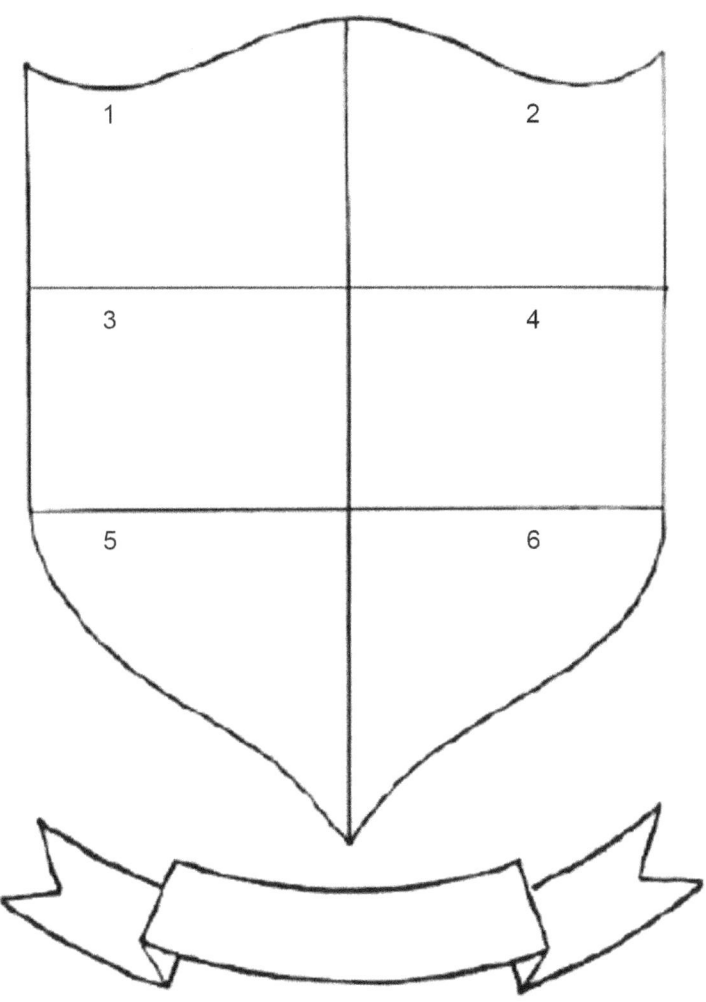

© 2018, Taylor & Francis, *Integrating SEL into Your Curriculum*,
John Dacey, Gian Criscitiello, and Maureen Devlin

Engage: Remind students that being aware of their own strengths increases their capability to work with others and display leadership qualities. Tell students that they will be creating personal shields that will display what makes them proud to be themselves. Shields were a historical way that families shared their accomplishments and strengths so that others could interact with them.

Activate: Pass out **Reproducible 11D1: Personal Shield**. Tell the students that they are going to use the shield to celebrate what makes them special. Have them make a symbol or drawing for each portion of the shield that matches the following list.

1. The happiest event of your life.
2. The greatest achievement in your life.
3. Something that you are good at.
4. Another thing that you are good at.
5. Something you would like to do or be someday.
6. Something you'd like to become better at.

Reflect: When finished, have students share their shields with a partner and ask if they can learn something new about someone. Use the following questions to lead a discussion:

- Was it hard for you to think of ideas for your shield?
- Were you surprised by what people put on their shields?
- Did you learn something new about someone today?
- Will these shields help you remember your strengths if we display them in the classroom?

ACTIVITY 11E Self-Care Is Not Selfish

AL Goal: Literacy Writing point-of-view paragraphs.

SEL Goal: Self-Awareness Understand the difference between taking care of oneself and being selfish.

Materials Needed: **Reproducible 11E1: Self-Care Versus Selfish**; pencil/pen

REPRODUCIBLE 11E1

Self-Care Versus Selfish

Directions: List as many things as you can think of for each column.

Caring for Yourself	Selfish

Engage: Discuss with students the two ideas of Self-Care and Selfishness. Ask them to think of what they may have heard about these ideas.

Activate: Pass out **Reproducible 11E1: Self-Care Versus Selfish**. Ask students to think about what it means to care for one's self. Have them fill out the column with any words, thoughts, or images that come to mind when they think of the phrase, "taking care of one's self." Then ask them to think about what it means for someone to be selfish. Have them fill out the column with anything that comes to mind with they hear the word "selfish." When they are done, have the students choose one of the columns and have them imagine they are either a person who practices self-care or a person who is selfish. Ask them to write a paragraph describing a typical daily event, such as lunch, from the point of view of that person.

Reflect: Have the students share their paragraphs. Lead a discussion using the following questions as a guide:

- What kinds of things did the self-care people do?
- What kinds of things did the selfish people do?
- What are some benefits to being someone who is practicing self-care?
- What are some benefits to being someone who is selfish?
- What are some things that you might do now to take care of yourself?
- Why is it important to take care of yourself?

Notes

1 Stevens, 2015, p. 1.
2 Salzberg, 2013, p. 5.
3 Goleman et al., 2013, p. 210.
4 Ryan, 2012, p. 116.
5 Ryan, 2012, p. 169.
6 Goleman et al., 2013, p. 225.
7 Walsh, 2013.
8 Nhat Hanh, 2008, p. 12.
9 Goleman et al., 2013, p. 235.

Part V
Responsible Decision-Making

12

Think Creatively

Every child is an artist. The problem is staying an artist when you grow up.
—Pablo Picasso

A lot of people forget how important it is to be creative. We get caught up in getting ahead and in day-to-day minutiae. But creativity is a fundamental mode of expression, as is being tenacious and standing by your own convictions and passions, even if it's not the "popular" choice.
—Tabatha Coffey

To be considered creative, must a person's achievements bring widespread recognition? We do not think so. As Schank and Cleary point out, simply getting through a typical day in the modern world requires imagination. "These small acts of creativity, though they differ in scope, are not different in kind from the brilliant leaps of an Einstein. Creativity is commonplace in cognition, not an esoteric gift bequeathed only to a few."[1]

So what do we know about ordinary creativity? First of all, it is not now and probably never was equally distributed throughout the world. As Zhao reports:

> There were less than 10 major inventions between 1 AD and 1800 AD. Contrast that to the last 200 years, during which time we have seen the creation of more than 25 life-altering technological and social inventions, such as computers, antibiotics, airplanes, internet, genetic engineering, organ transplants, automobiles, lasers, and telecommunication. Consider this: if you had been born more than 2,000 years

ago it would have been possible to live your entire life without being impacted by a life-changing invention. When you live in the 21st century, a time fraught with change, that's pretty hard to imagine.[2]

At the present time, education in Western societies has swung toward content knowledge and its evaluation by standardized tests. In Eastern societies, where content knowledge was prominent for centuries, a more equitable balance between the two goals is being sought. As recent research has found,

> Chinese student scores on an annual international assessment of creativity have been rapidly rising since 1990, whereas American scores have been decreasing. The test is considered valid by scholars, and has a high correlation with success later in life.[3]

ACTIVITY 12A What's in the Box?

AL Goal: Literacy Describe in-depth a character, setting, or event in a story or drama, drawing on specific details in the text (e.g., a character's thoughts, words, or actions).

SEL Goal: Responsible Decision-Making Choosing the right character, setting, or event to create a high-quality story in a limited amount of time.

Materials Needed: paper and pencil; **Reproducible 12A1: Maxie**

REPRODUCIBLE 12A1

Maxie

© 2018, Taylor & Francis, *Integrating SEL into Your Curriculum*,
John Dacey, Gian Criscitiello, and Maureen Devlin

Engage: Tell your students to write a story about the scene in **Reproducible 12A1: Maxie**. There is no right way to write it. Be as imaginative as you can! (Allow 10 minutes).

Activate: You might want to mention the following study to the class. In their research on imaginative problem-solving, John Dacey and Richard Ripple[4] evaluated the stories about this picture of 1,200 fourth through eighth grade students. Amazingly, about 900 of the stories were almost exactly alike! (They were about how the animal's curiosity became its undoing). The other 300 stories, however, were decidedly different from each other. Here is one of those stories by a fifth-grader:

A Tail [sic] About a Frighted [sic] Chipmunk

> Artie, the chipmunk, was chasing a beetle. He was starving.
> The sky above him was dark and stormy. The leafy ground in the forest was smelly. Artie wondered how he was going to get any food. He thought of last night and the monsters. Some had four sharp claws, others had huge round eyes. Joe was so scared!
> Suddenly a bear jumped out of the bushes . . . (the story ends because time ran out.)

The students who wrote the better stories frequently used the small square in the picture merely as a departure point from which they could travel to other, more exotic lands. Many saw it as a window or a door through which they could leave the simple scene. Others stretched their imaginations to describe it as a time capsule, a case of TNT, a casket, or a player piano. A small number disregarded the square altogether.

Reflect: Ask students to answer two simple questions:

1. "Honestly, was your story more like the 900 ordinary ones, or the 300 extraordinary ones?"
2. "Knowing what you know now, would you like to try again?"

ACTIVITY 12B What Do You Notice? What Do You Wonder?

AL Goal: STEAM Reasoning about shapes and their attributes.

SEL Goal: Relationship Skills Improve interpersonal problem-solving skills.

Materials Needed: paper and pencil; **Reproducible 12B1: Circles within Circles; Reproducible 12B2: Two More Circles within Circles**

REPRODUCIBLE 12B1

Circles within Circles

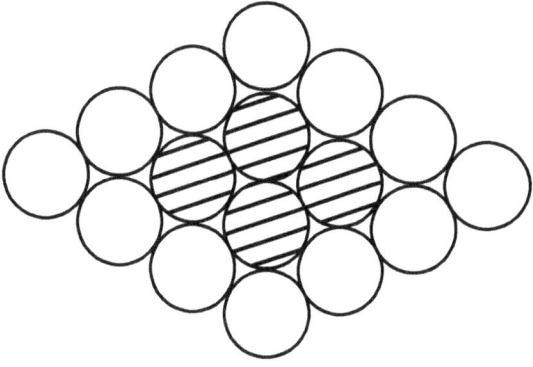

© 2018, Taylor & Francis, *Integrating SEL into Your Curriculum*,
John Dacey, Gian Criscitiello, and Maureen Devlin

REPRODUCIBLE 12B2

Two More Circles within Circles

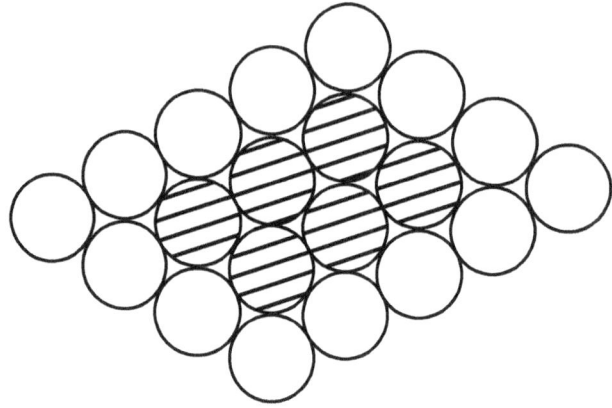

© 2018, Taylor & Francis, *Integrating SEL into Your Curriculum*,
John Dacey, Gian Criscitiello, and Maureen Devlin

Engage: Show students **Reproducible 12B1: Circles within Circles**.

Activate: In this activity, they should try to notice all the aspects of a geometric figure. Examples of what they might come up with are:

- Outside shape is a diamond.
- Inside shape is a diamond.
- There are four shaded circles.
- There are 12 open circles.
- You can see a lot of triangles within this picture.

To promote this type of creative thinking, the National Council of Teachers of Mathematics suggest that you "create a safe environment where students focus on sharing their thoughts without any pressure to solve a problem."[5]

Reflect: Now you want them to wonder. Ask them to think what would happen if two more shaded circles were added inside to blank circles. Show them **Reproducible 12B2: Two More Circles within Circles**. Ask how many blank circles you need to add to enclose the shaded circles again? (The answer is two.)

Now ask about adding 38 shaded circles—how many open circles do you need to add to enclose the shaded circles again? Many students will try to figure this out by actually drawing the circles. (The answer is 38; you always need to add the same number of open circles as the number of shaded circles you have added). Ask them if they notice a relationship between the number of shaded circles and open circles. Can they think of a simple formula for answering this question? Ask if they can think of any other questions. (One might be what happens to the diamond shape when you add shaded circles—the shape becomes a parallelogram.)

ACTIVITY 12C Litter-ally

AL Goal: STEAM Collect data scientifically, graph it, and write a cogent report.

SEL Goal: Social Awareness Using imagination to better understand human behavior.

Materials Needed: paper and pencil; 10 pieces of string, each one-yard-long; large garbage bags, one for every three children in your class; **Reproducible 12C1: Types of Litter**

REPRODUCIBLE 12C1

Types of Litter

Types of litter	Children	Teenagers	Adults	Anyone
Bottles				
Cans				
Plastic bags				
School papers				
Candy wrappers				
Other food wrappers				
Other items, list here:				
Totals:				

© 2018, Taylor & Francis, *Integrating SEL into Your Curriculum*, John Dacey, Gian Criscitiello, and Maureen Devlin

Engage: The purpose of this activity is to help students assess the litter problem around their school, and if you choose, other areas in the neighborhood. They will use creative thinking to solve a problem by inferring who is responsible for the litter. By noting the number of hours the students have devoted to this process, the cost to the town (if town workers have been employed) can also be calculated.

Explain to the students that you are going to show them how to collect data about litter around their school. They are going to categorize the data, graph it, and make a report to the Department of Public Works in hopes of reducing the unsightly problem.

Activate: Show them **Reproducible 12C1: Types of Litter**. This will be the form they will use to collect their data for the report. You might begin this research by discussing the meaning of the word "litter." When the students have agreed on a definition, tell them to use the following steps to collect the data:

1. Have them count off by threes.
2. The groups are to go into the schoolyard and find different areas of litter.
3. One student in each group should hold out his arms to define the collection area. It should not overlap with anyone else's collection area.
4. Use one piece of string to define a circle on the ground around his feet approximately one yard in diameter.
5. Using one of the garbage bags, collect all the litter in that circle.

Reflect: Bring the litter inside and categorize it, using **Reproducible 12C1: Types of Litter**. At least two of the students must agree on the category of each item. Combine all of the small group reports into one master report and a copy of **Reproducible 12C1**. When the master data sheet is completed, explain to the students how to graph the data.

Now they need to work together to prepare a document on their findings to the Department of Public Works. An important part of this report will be their determination of which age group is mainly responsible for the litter. They should brainstorm ideas that need to go into the report, and then elect a committee of five students to prepare it. It should be sent to the superintendent of the Public Works Department, and then a meeting with her should be arranged. Finally, this committee should report back to the class on what actions the superintendent said would be taken.

ACTIVITY 12D Creatively Matching Ideas

AL Goal: ELA Using word association to increase vocabulary.

SEL Goal: Self-Awareness Becoming more aware of one's creative abilities through a cognitive challenge.

Materials Needed: paper and pencil; **Reproducible 12D1: Pairing Challenge; Reproducible 12D2: Answers to the Pairing Challenge**

REPRODUCIBLE 12D1

Pairing Challenge

In this exercise, you are presented with three words and asked to find a fourth word that is related to those three. Note: the first three words have little to do with each other, but all three ARE associated with the fourth word. That is the one you are to guess. For example, what word do you think is related to these three?

    cookies sugar heart _____

The answer in this case is "sweet." Cookies are sweet; so is sugar, and sweet is part of the word "sweetheart."

    Here is another example: fast go molasses _____

You should have written the word "slow" in the answer space, because it goes with each of the other words. "Slow" is the opposite of "fast," it's part of the phrase "go slow," and also a part of the phrase "slow as molasses." As you can see, the fourth word can be related to the other three for different reasons. You really have to use your imagination!

    Now try these sets of three words. Write the word you think is correct in the space following the three words. Don't spend too much time trying to get any one answer. You have seven minutes.

1. Jill — tire — beanstalk — _____
2. mountain — low — skyscraper — _____
3. package — cardboard — ring — _____
4. surprise — presents — birthday — _____
5. crazy — salted — pecan — _____
6. connect — high — electric — _____
7. butterfly — catch — fish — _____
8. sun — bulb — heavy — _____
9. slit — knife — Band-Aid — _____
10. snow — color — black — _____
11. building — house — plate — _____
12. slugger — wood — ball — _____
13. stage — game — actor — _____
14. Roman — arithmetic — VII — _____
15. cat — white — dark — _____
16. round — bat — beach — _____

© 2018, Taylor & Francis, *Integrating SEL into Your Curriculum*,
John Dacey, Gian Criscitiello, and Maureen Devlin

Answers to the Pairing Challenge

1. jack
2. high
3. box
4. party
5. nut
6. wire
7. net
8. light
9. cut
10. white
11. home
12. bat
13. play
14. numeral
15. black
16. ball

Engage: Present **Reproducible 12D1: Pairing Challenge.**

Activate: After seven minutes, ask students to swap answers with another pupil, then read the answers. Tell them you will bet that for any one item, at least one student will have gotten the right answer. After scoring, ask if anyone got them all right.

Reflect: Pass out or read from the answer sheet, **Reproducible 12D2: Answers to the Pairing Challenge**. Explain that creativity is the process by which ideas already in the mind are paired in unusual and useful combinations. Every image or concept we have is associated with other images and concepts. When people think about solving a problem, they mentally cast about for an association that might serve as a solution. Most of us accept the first idea that seems to solve the problem. Creative people are those who go further down the mental list, searching for more unusual but higher-quality pairings to solve their problems. It is these remote pairings that produce creative ideas.

Now ask students to discuss the following questions:

- Do you believe this is a fair test of creativity?
- Do you think your score represents your actual ability?
- What are some reasons we might want to measure creative ability with a simple test like this?

ACTIVITY 12E Lateral Thinking

AL Goal: ELA Understand and invent sayings (adages, maxims, proverbs) in imaginative, unique ways.

SEL Goal: Social Awareness What common sayings indicate about us human beings.

Materials Needed: paper and pencil; **Reproducible 12E1: Common Sayings (Animals); Reproducible 12E2: Some Other Common Sayings**

(Teacher: Answers to **Reproducible 12E1: Common Sayings (Animals)**: bird; mice; chickens; duck's; bees; fish)

REPRODUCIBLE 12E1

Common Sayings (Animals)

1. A _____ in the hand is worth two in the bush.
2. When the cat's away the _____ will play.
3. Don't count your _____ before they are hatched.
4. Like water off a _____ back.
5. You can catch more _____ with honey than you can with vinegar.
6. There are plenty of _____ in the sea.

© 2018, Taylor & Francis, *Integrating SEL into Your Curriculum*,
John Dacey, Gian Criscitiello, and Maureen Devlin

REPRODUCIBLE 12E2

Some Other Common Sayings

A fool and his money are soon parted.
It takes one to know one.
Better late than never.
An apple doesn't fall far from the tree.

Engage: Lateral thinking is typical "outside the box" creative thinking used when a straight-ahead, linear, step-by-step approach may not be as productive. Tell students the game they are going to play promotes something called "lateral thinking." It uses such common sayings as, "You can get more bees with honey than with vinegar." Here are some others they might try (**Reproducible 12E1: Common Sayings (Animals))**.

Activate: As another example, pass out **Reproducible 12E2: Some Other Common Sayings**. Think of as many of these adages as possible, and write down the first part of each on a 3 by 5 card. For example, you would write down "The apple doesn't fall . . ." or, "It takes one to . . ." The point of this game is to come up with funny endings.

Put all your cards in a brown paper bag. Each player chooses a card from the bag and then has 15 seconds to come up with a different, funny ending for the saying. For example, if you pick "The apple doesn't fall . . ." you might come up with the ending ". . . if you're holding onto it really tight."

Reflect: After all the cards are used, discuss which of the endings each of you found the funniest. Answer the question, "What has this got to do with creativity?"

Now that you have some models to follow, we hope you will spend a lot of time nurturing your students' creativity. Our planet needs you to do so—desperately!

Notes

1 Schank and Cleary, 1995, p. 229.
2 Zhao, 2014, p. 1.
3 "The Creativity Crisis," July, 2010.
4 Dacey and Ripple, 1969, p. 323.
5 NCTM, 2016, p. 1.

13

Think Critically and Wisely

Standardized testing is at cross purposes with many of the most important purposes of public education. It doesn't measure big-picture learning, critical thinking, perseverance, problem solving, creativity or curiosity, yet those are the qualities great teaching brings out in a student.

—Randi Weingarten

Common Core reminds us what testing can do right. Modeled on standards of the world's education superpowers, questions demand critical thinking and creativity. Students are asked to write at length, show their work, and explain their reasoning.

—Wendy Kopp

These two statements contradict each other, or seem to. Which one most reflects your experience? More to the point of this chapter, how would a good critical thinker react? When we asked our teacher-advisors about which of these two viewpoints were most true, they agreed that it *depends* on the system. They recognized that the veracity of a statement relies on the context about which it is made. Both are sometimes true, but they all agreed the first one applies most of the time. Hence this book.

So what is critical thinking, exactly? The term means "the intellectually disciplined process of actively and skillfully conceptualizing, applying, analyzing, synthesizing, and/or evaluating information gathered from, or generated by, observation, experience, reflection, reasoning, or communication, as a guide to belief and action."[1] Whew. That's a mouthful! Here's another definition: the awakening of the intellect to the study of itself.[2] That, we think, is the heart of critical thinking. It differs from independent thinking in that it relies more on logic, and less on social relations.

The opposite of critical thinking is murky and irrational thought. Current educational practices in too many classrooms around the planet tend to promote cautious, compliant memorization, as opposed to bold reflection. This leaves many students feeling fuzzy-headed and uninspired. When children enhance their social and emotional skills, their interest in academic skills improves as well. In simple terms, critical thinking examines assumptions and biases (WHY?), discerns hidden values and evaluates evidence (WHAT?), and assesses conclusions *(HOW?)*. Educator Ian Gilbert offers a simple recommendation: "Open minds to question, to reflect, to look beneath the surface, to have beliefs that they will fight for and fight for the beliefs of others, even if they don't agree with them."[3]

ACTIVITY 13A Mystery Boxes

AL Goal: STEAM Generate and compare multiple possible solutions to a problem based on how well each is likely to meet the criteria and constraints of the problem.

SEL Goal: Responsible Decision-Making Make predictions based on information gained objectively from using one's senses. Learn to look at and use data as scientists do.

Materials Needed: three small boxes, such as 3" × 5" cardboard jewelry boxes, or boxes that can be recycled from home (such as those originally containing instant oatmeal packets, granola bars, or macaroni and cheese. If using recycled boxes, it is helpful to cover the boxes with construction paper or brown paper bag paper in order to make them look the same); an assortment of small objects such as marshmallows, dry macaroni, buttons, paper clips, and pennies (whatever you have around); tape.

Before you begin the activity, prepare the boxes so that each box contains several of the same objects inside. Tape each box closed securely so that no objects can fall out if the box is shaken. You may want to make several identical boxes if you will be doing this activity in groups.

Engage: Tell students they will be using their senses and judgment to try to guess what objects are in each of these boxes. Say that you want them to use whatever senses they prefer to learn the traits of the objects in the box.

Activate: As they explore the boxes, ask students to explain the difference between what they actually sense and what they infer. For example, "The box has more than one object inside it" or "Whatever is inside must be quite small" can be sensed. An inference would be something like, "It seems like the objects might be cotton balls." While observations can be supported by evidence and facts, inferences are not as clear and can be arrived at through deducing from what is sensed.

Reflect: After several different observations have been recorded, ask them:

- What is your best guess about what is in the box? How about a prediction?
- What makes you think so?
- How confident are you about your prediction?
- If they disagree, ask them to think of the best way they could resolve it.
- Regardless of whether each group's hypothesis is right or wrong, ask students, "What does any of this have to do with critical thinking?" (For example, were some of the students dissuaded from their answers by another self-assured student?)

ACTIVITY 13B Common Thinking Errors

AL Goal: STEAM (Psychology) Determine the correctness of statements by analyzing them with common thinking traps in mind.

SEL Goal: Responsible Decision-Making Learn to avoid common thinking traps when making choices.

Materials Needed: paper and pencil; **Reproducible 13B1: Common Thinking Traps**

Common Thinking Traps

1. *Telescopic vision*—looking at things through one end or the other of the telescope makes them seem bigger or smaller than they really are.

2. *Black-and-white thinking*—looking at things in only extreme or opposite ways (e.g., good or bad, never or always, all or none).

3. *Dark glasses*—thinking about only the negative side of the matter (also called "*catastrophizing*").

4. *Fortune telling*—making predictions about what will happen in the future without enough evidence.

5. *Making it too personal*—blaming self for things that aren't your fault.

6. *Blame game*—blaming others for things for which you should take responsibility.[4]

Engage: Explain to students that one of the benefits of being able to think critically is that it helps us avoid some common thinking errors or traps. These are ways of viewing situations through lenses that inevitably make us feel insecure. Being able to discern such situations accurately will help your child avoid falling into harmful habits of mind.

Activate: Pass out **Reproducible 13B1: Common Thinking Traps**. Ask your students to try and think of examples from their own lives of one of these thinking traps.

Reflect: Request that they be really honest and tell the class one of their examples. Ask each student to participate, but allow anyone who wants to take a pass. After each example, inquire what the student believes she should have done or thought differently. Also after each example, inquire whether any students have other recommendations for avoiding critical thinking traps.

ACTIVITY 13C Searching for Meanings

AL Goal: STEAM Solve problems involving four operations, and identify and explain patterns in arithmetic.

SEL Goal: Responsible Decision-Making Make use of multiple strategies leading to insightful decision-making.

Materials Needed: pencil; **Reproducible 13C1: Searching for Meanings (Teacher's Version of Possible Answers)**; **Reproducible 13C2: Searching for Meanings (Student's Version)**

REPRODUCIBLE 13C1

Searching for Meanings (Teacher's Version of Possible Answers)

1. All are factors of 40. (1 x 40, 2 x 20, 4 x 10, 5 x 8).
2. Only one factor is odd. Why?
3. What about seven other even numbers?
4. There are eight factors, which is even. Meaningful?
5. The factors add up 90.
6. Subtract to –10.
7. Multiply to 2,560,000.

REPRODUCIBLE 13C2

Searching for Meanings (Student's Version)

What do you notice about the number series 1, 2, 4, 5, 8, 10, 20, and 40? What do you wonder about the relationships among these numbers?

1. _____.
2. _____.
3. _____.
4. _____.
5. _____.
6. _____.
7. _____.
8. _____.
9. _____.
10. _____.

© 2018, Taylor & Francis, *Integrating SEL into Your Curriculum*,
John Dacey, Gian Criscitiello, and Maureen Devlin

Engage: Explain to your students that critical thinking requires them to use their ability to reason. However, using their reason often requires the ability to wonder, to wander around a problem aimlessly, to think laterally (see Chapter 12).

Activate: Pass out **Reproducible 13C2: Searching for Meanings (Student's Version)** to each student. Give them an appropriate amount of time to respond.

Reflect: Ask them to form groups of four and share what they have on their answer sheets. Then ask them to discuss the following questions:

1. Ask yourself, "What method did I use to come up with my answers?"
2. "Can we put our answers into categories?"
3. Looking at each student's answers, ask "Can you see any methods you tended to use in solving the problem?"
4. "Were there correct answers to this problem? How can you tell them from wrong answers?"
5. "This is an exercise in critical thinking; can you see how?"

ACTIVITY 13D Triangle Challenge

AL Goal: STEAM Geometric measurement: recognize perimeter as an attribute of plane figures.

SEL Goal: Responsible Decision-Making Learning to have an open, creative mind when attempting to solve problems.

Materials Needed: two different colored pencils; **Reproducible 13D1: Don't Finish It!**

REPRODUCIBLE 13D1

Don't Finish It!

· · · · ·

· · · · ·

· · · · ·

· · · · ·

· · · · ·

© 2018, Taylor & Francis, *Integrating SEL into Your Curriculum*,
John Dacey, Gian Criscitiello, and Maureen Devlin

Engage: Pass out **Reproducible 13D1: Don't Finish It!** Tell students to look at the handout, then ask them to try to guess what it is for. Push for as many guesses as you can get.

Activate: Tell students that the goal of this activity is simple—to avoid adding the third line of a triangle by connecting the dots. Pair them up into groups of two and then explain that you want each student to take turns connecting two dots into a line. As lines are formed, they will eventually create some triangles. If they connect the final line to form a triangle, then they must put the first letter of their name inside the triangle. The person with the most triangles with their initial in the middle loses the game.

Reflect: As they progress through this activity, you should encourage them to think creatively. For example, a triangle need not only be three segments big. It could be 3 dots long by 3 dots long by 3 dots long, or 4 dots by 4 dots by 4 dots, and so on. The two different colored pencils will help indicate who has discovered the many varying triangles. While it is certainly fun to see who establishes the most triangles, you should learn about their minds by seeing how creatively different triangles can be identified and how one person might see a triangle while the other doesn't.

ACTIVITY 13E True, False, or Maybe?

From social media to cable TV, it's easy to find ourselves in information silos of our own construction, getting news and views from likeminded sources, and shutting ourselves off from perspectives that might surprise or challenge us. This reality—call it an echo chamber or a filter bubble—can make it hard to grapple with the complexities of the world we live in.

—Bob Cohn

AL Goal: Literacy and *STEAM* To analyze word and number problems to get at the truth. To develop the ability to make decisions based on facts, rather than on assumptions or popular ideas.

SEL Goal: Responsible Decision-Making To make good decisions on the basis of social and emotional data, as well as academic data.

Materials Needed: pencil/pen; **Reproducible 13E1: Fact or Opinion? (Teacher's Version of Possible Answers)**; **Reproducible 13E2: Fact or Opinion? (Student's Version).**

REPRODUCIBLE 13E1

Fact or Opinion? (Teacher's Version of Possible Answers)

- Christopher Columbus discovered America (false: he actually landed on various Caribbean islands and the coasts of Central and South America, but never set foot on the land we know as the United States of America).
- You use only 10% of your brain (maybe: we cannot say what percentage of our brains we use. That would require us to know what it would be like to use 100% of our brain. No one knows that. We use regions of the brain in different ways doing different tasks, and not necessarily all at once or to the same extent).
- The expressions 3x+5 and 5x+3 are equal (maybe, but only when x=1).
- Storks deliver babies (true: their own but not humans).
- Four out of five dentists studied choose Colgate Toothpaste (maybe: depends on whether the researcher cheated and mostly used dentists who were known to favor Colgate).
- The product of multiplied numbers is larger than either the multiplier or the multiplicand (Maybe, but not when one of them is a fraction).
- That short person over there is the son of the tall person standing next to him, but the tall person is not the short person's father (true: the tall person is the short person's mother).
- Make up your own:

- Make up your own:

Fact or Opinion? (Student's Version)

- Christopher Columbus discovered America. True____ False____ Maybe____
- You use only 10% of your brain. True____ False____ Maybe____
- The expressions 3x+5 and 5x+3 are equal. True____ False____ Maybe____
- Storks deliver babies. True____ False____ Maybe____
- Four out of five dentists studied choose Colgate Toothpaste. True____ False____ Maybe____
- The product of multiplied numbers is larger than either the multiplier or the multiplicand. True____ False____ Maybe____
- That short person over there is the son of the tall person standing next to him, but the tall person is not the short person's father. True____ False____ Maybe____
- Make up your own: True____ False____ Maybe____
- Make up your own: True____ False____ Maybe____

Engage: Ask your students to pause and think about how often their beliefs result from popular opinion or even false myths. An important step in critical thinking is, "Think again!" Tell them that to be a good thinker, they should always ask themselves, "This seems to be true (or false), but could it be just the opposite? And sometimes, maybe, the answer is, maybe."

Activate: Now pass out **Reproducible 13E2: Fact or Opinion? (Student's Version)** and ask them to fill out the answer space for each statement as to whether it is true, false, or maybe.

Reflect: By this stage, your students should know how to reflect on their own thinking. So ask them to make up their own reflection tasks.

ACTIVITY 13F All, Some, or None—Bonus Activity

AL Goal: Literacy and *STEAM* To analyze data in a photograph to get at the truth. To develop the ability to make decisions based on the meanings of words, on facts, rather than on assumptions.

SEL Goal: Responsible Decision-Making To discern the accuracy of statements.

Materials Needed: pencil/pen; **Reproducible 13F1: Puppy Heaven**; **Reproducible 13F2: Puppy Heaven: All, Some or None**

REPRODUCIBLE 13F1

Puppy Heaven

© 2018, Taylor & Francis, *Integrating SEL into Your Curriculum*,
John Dacey, Gian Criscitiello, and Maureen Devlin

REPRODUCIBLE 13F2

Puppy Heaven: All, Some or None

Answer the following questions about the picture entitled "Puppy Heaven" with the word "All," "Some," or "None."

1. _____ of the dogs have patches.
2. _____ of the dogs have black noses.
3. _____ of the dogs are red.
4. _____ of the dogs are sitting on their back paws.
5. _____ of the dogs have ears that stick out
6. _____ of the dogs are touching another dog.
7. _____ of the dogs are asleep.
8. _____ of the dogs are brownish tan.

© 2018, Taylor & Francis, *Integrating SEL into Your Curriculum*,
John Dacey, Gian Criscitiello, and Maureen Devlin

Engage: Pass out **Reproducible 13F1: Puppy Heaven**.

Activate: Next pass out **Reproducible 13F2: Puppy Heaven: All, Some, or None**.

Reflect: By this stage, your students should know how to reflect on their own thinking, so ask them to make up their own reflection tasks.

Notes

1 Scriven and Paul, Summer 1987, p. 1.
2 Scriven and Paul, Summer 1987, p. 1.
3 Gilbert, 2014.
4 Merrell and Gueldner, 2010.

Part VI
Achieving Teaching Goals More Effectively

14

Help for Harried Teachers

It's very hard to balance being there for somebody else and taking care of yourself.

—Jennifer Grey

Technology is just a tool. In terms of getting the kids working together and motivating them, the teacher is the most important.

—Bill Gates

"Being a community member is part of what it means to be authentic."[1] The author of this quotation reinforces anthropologist Margaret Mead's famous view: "Never doubt that a small group of thoughtful, committed citizens can change the world; indeed it's the only thing that ever has."[2]

Most efforts to strengthen social and emotional skills in schools are designed to include all students, even though 80% of the students do not have mental health problems. They also involve protective factors, such as "a positive and caring school climate, development of positive relationships between students and their teachers, and effective academic instructional planning."[3] The underlying idea here is one of synergy, where two interventions delivered simultaneously—in the home and in the school—have greater impact.

The focus of this chapter is to suggest actions that will connect you with:

- People in similar positions of authority—parents, caregivers, teachers, and administrators.
- Researchers and writers who regularly share current information in education.

- National organizations striving to advance children's education and social and emotional well-being.
- Publications and additional resources to further your own learning and to share with others.
- Strategies to enhance students' social and emotional skills in general.

Psychologist Shefali Tsabary advises: "True giving, which is fundamentally different from giving because it fills an empty space in your life and is therefore a form of neediness, comes from awareness of inner abundance. There is no giving if the inner well is dry. Authentic giving originates from a well that overflows."[4]

ACTION 14A Reflect, Read, and Research

John Dewey's popular quote, "We do not learn from experience . . . we learn from reflecting on experience," provides educators with the first step to organizing their efforts. Margaret Mead's maxim, "Without reflection, we go blindly on our way, creating more unintended consequences, and failing to achieve anything useful,"[5] further supports Dewey's words. To avoid becoming harried, an educator's first task is to make time for reflection.

Educators today often reflect publicly with online blogging, YouTube videos, Ted Talks, and podcasts. The advantage is that you receive feedback, which spurs more reflection and subsequent action.

Multiple books guide educators about reflection. Organizations such as the Association for Supervision and Curriculum Development (ASCD), The National Council of Teachers of English (NCTE), National Council of Teachers of Mathematics (NCTM), and the Association for Experiential Education (AEE) provide step-by-step guides, rationale, and research related to reflection. Two other examples:

Teach100

Teach100 ranks and scores hundreds of education blogs. This is a great resource for educators to review in order to "hear" the voices of other educators as they reflect on their craft and share their experiences and research.

Bam Radio

Bam Radio is an online resource that aims to "amplify the voices of the education village." This resource provides educators with access to education podcasts, blog posts, and radio shows. Bam Radio also shares its reflections and research via its many platforms.

ACTION 14B Establish a Professional Learning Network (PLN)

Thanks to the numerous social networking sites such as Facebook, Twitter, Voxer, and Instagram, many educator support groups exist solely online. Such groups provide forums for educators to come together around one or more common interests regardless of geographical location, and offer rich opportunities for sharing ideas, advice, and resources.

Many websites feature discussion and/or message boards so that visitors to the site can discuss information, concerns, and opinions. These boards range from those that function like bulletin boards, where visitors post messages that others can see (one-way communication), to discussion forums that occur in *asynchronous* or *synchronous* fashion. An asynchronous discussion forum means that visitors can post comments or questions at any time, and someone can respond at another time. Synchronous discussion forums occur at specific times when participants can post and respond in the moment, often bringing people into contact from around the world.

One of the most obvious sources for support and validation for educators is other educators. A relationship with even one other teacher is all that it takes to reduce your own anxiety and elevate your craft. There are many opportunities to meet other teachers, including virtual and real time groups inside and outside the school community. The following sites are popular places for educators and others to explore, and most do not require any fees for the use of their platforms:

Facebook: www.facebook.com

Once you have established a free Facebook account, you can look to the "Groups" link on the left-hand menu. There are icons to "Create Group" and "Find New Groups," and you are able to adjust your privacy settings (e.g., who can see your personal information) by clicking on the icon that looks like a padlock with three little lines. The site is user-friendly, and there are also many online tips available outside of the Facebook site for those who have the time and inclination to explore the Internet for Facebook-inspired ideas.

Pinterest: www.pinterest.com

This site functions like an interactive bulletin board, allowing users to "pin" websites to their own accounts. For example, suppose you search for "healthy snacks" and find a recipe for creative school snacks. To save this recipe, you may "pin" it to your "board." You are able to create your boards, almost like file folders, where your different pinned websites are available as snapshots for you to look at. You are also able to "follow" friends and others on Pinterest, and can therefore connect with others around specific interests or activities. There are numerous sites to explore related to teaching on Pinterest, featuring tips, humor, and forums for exchange.

Edmodo: www.edmodo.com

This site is specifically designed to bring teachers, families, and students together in the spirit of sharing. This site is particularly useful for professionals—teachers and administrators; Edmodo is a secure website that offers many opportunities for engagement. The detailed set of instructions walks users through the process of connecting with others on a specific topic or for continued professional development.

Twitter: https://twitter.com

Thousands of educators have Twitter accounts and regularly share information via Twitter chats and tweets. Popular Twitter chats can be found via www.iste.org/explore/articledetail?articleid=7

Educators generally post their picture, a link to their blog and/or website, and a short description of their professional work and personal interests. They share links to good ideas, blog posts, images, video, and other educational resources, ideas, and questions related to good teaching.

Discovery Education: www.discoveryeducation.com/

This is a popular education site that has numerous teaching/learning resources and an online community of educators that eagerly share ideas.

Voxer: https://web.voxer.com/login

Many educators exchange ideas on this audial social media thread. Similar to Twitter and Facebook, Voxer provides educators with a place to share ideas. It's unique in that the ideas are shared via speaking rather than writing or sharing images. Many educators prefer this vehicle.

Google+: https://plus.google.com

Google+ is Google's social network. It is a network that is easily coordinated with the Google apps and accounts that you establish. Similar to Facebook and Twitter, Google+ consists of a stream of updates, conversations, and shared contact. You add your contacts to "circles," which provides a way to categorize and organize people. You may comment on people's shares and also utilize the "Hangout" feature to video chat. There's a smart phone Google+ app as well.

ACTION 14C Education Publications

Many organizations provide links to publications and resources that you may find useful and want to share with colleagues, relatives, and other learning community members:

The Inner Resilience Program: www.innerresilience-tidescenter.org/publications.html

Defending the Early Years: http://deyproject.org/recommended-reading-and-resources/

Schools that Learn: http://schoolsthatlearn.com

Mindful Schools: www.mindfulschools.org

Edutopia: www.edutopia.org/

MindShift: http://ww2.kqed.org/mindshift/

Classroom Q&A With Larry Ferlazzo Website: http://blogs.edweek.org/teachers/classroom_qa_with_larry_ferlazzo/

The Jose Vilson: http://thejosevilson.com/

ACTION 14D Get Involved in National and International Organizations

One of the quickest ways to get connected to others is by asking, "How can I get involved?" For example, The Bill and Melinda Gates Education Organization issued a Request for Proposal (RFP) for educators who wanted to host educator gatherings to Celebrate and Elevate Effective Teaching and Teachers in the United States. The events fostered collegiality, idea share, and support for educators. Education-related organizations and companies throughout the country support countless educator events that support teachers who want to get involved. Being able to help others very often results in helping oneself:

- Establish a network of responsible, reliable education supporters who are interested in working with teachers and schools.
- Form afterschool clubs related to specific content areas.
- Connect adults in professional clubs, workshops, and courses to create and/or build teaching/learning efforts in that area.
- Inspire advocacy and activism for professional endeavors. Work with local governmental, community, and/or union groups.

- Write proposals for grants and to provide professional learning workshops and conference sessions related to the content areas you are most interested in.

For detailed tips and guidelines for starting your own local support group, see the Edmodo website listed in Action 14B. The national organizations listed below provide support and outreach in this area. Most of these national organizations have local affiliations in each state and outside of the United States as well.

Collaborative for Academic, Social, and Emotional Learning: www.casel.org

Twitter: @caselorg

The leading organization in the United States for promoting SEL in preschool through high school, CASEL bases its advice entirely on evidence obtained in highly rigorous, widely respected research studies. The organization focuses its efforts and impact on research and policy.

Six Seconds: www.6seconds.org

Twitter: @6s_EQ

Six Seconds reaches people across the globe who are engaged in efforts to teach emotional intelligence skills. This organization helps children, families, schools, and other groups to succeed.

ASCD: The Whole Child: www.ascd.org

Twitter: @ASCD

The Association for Supervision and Child Development is an international presence in curriculum development, designed to empower educators, promote leadership, and support success for individual and group learners.

UNICEF: www.unicef.org

Twitter: @UNICEF

UNICEF is an organization dedicated to protecting the rights, health, and well-being of children around the world. They place particular emphasis on the early childhood years and children in the most vulnerable settings.

National Center on Safe & Supportive Learning Environments: https://safesupportivelearning.ed.gov

Twitter: @SSLearn

The NCSSLE addresses issues such as bullying, harassment, violence, and substance abuse in an effort to improve learning conditions for all students. Funded by the U.S. Department of Education, this organization provides training to students, teachers, communities and families, and administrators at various levels.

Character Education Partnership: http://character.org

Twitter: @CharacterDotOrg

This nonprofit organization envisions young people everywhere as educated, inspired, ethical, engaged citizens. Offering training, a national conference, and evaluation tools, the organization strives to connect educators and others who seek to improve school conditions.

National Parent-Teacher Association: www.pta.org

Twitter: @NationalPTA

For over 100 years, National PTA has been recognized as the premier organization that connects stakeholders in children's educational experiences—families, students, teachers, administrators, and community members. The work of the National PTA and its partners is promoted through publications, conferences, and social media venues.

National Institute of Mental Health: www.nimh.nih.gov

Twitter: @NIMHgov

Dedicated to transforming the understanding and treatment of mental illnesses, this national organization supports and disseminates research on a variety of topics. Scientific perspectives and applications of numerous findings are presented in links to publications, blogs, and video clips.

National Association of School Psychologists: nasponline.org

Twitter: @nasponline

NASP strives to empower school psychologists by promoting effective practices in the areas of advocacy, leadership, and cultural responsiveness.

National Council of Teachers of Mathematics (NCTM): www.nctm.org/

NCTM hosts countless links and resources related to math education and professional learning. Since most professional learning organizations are embedding SEL into their content work, you will likely find math resources that connect well with your desire to teach math and SEL at the same time.

National Education Association: www.nea.org/

This is a national teachers' union that has countless links to online communities for teacher connection, learning, and opportunity.

National Council of Teachers of English (NCTE): www.ncte.org/

This is the organization that supports teaching and learning in the area of English Language Arts.

International Society for Technology in Education (ISTE): www.iste.org/

A global community of educators supporting the use of technology to teach and learn.

National Board of Professional Teaching Standards (NBPTS): www.nbpts.org/

This national board works to strengthen the teaching profession and improve student learning by establishing high standards for teachers in American schools. Obtaining NBPTS certification promotes extensive educator reflection which leads to improved teaching, learning, and professional connections.

National Council of Social Studies (NCSS): www.socialstudies.org/

National council to foster teaching and learning in social studies. For many schools, social studies is the curriculum area where SEL is mainly embedded. Therefore this is a rich resource for the combined content and SEL teaching and learning.

Center for Teaching Quality (CTQ): www.teachingquality.org/

CTQ is a research-based, nonprofit advocacy organization that focuses primarily on the conditions of teaching with the vision of a high-quality public education system for all students, driven by the bold ideas and expert practices of teachers. Their mission is to connect, ready, and mobilize teacher/leaders to transform schools.

National Science Teachers Association (NSTA): www.nsta.org/

National association related to teaching and learning in science. With most educators in the country working to learn and teach new science standards, this is a rich resource for interdisciplinary SEL and science teaching.

ACTION 14E Take Advantage of Professional Learning Seminars and Conferences

There are countless professional learning seminars and conferences hosted by educational organizations, local school systems, universities, and other professional organizations. Most of these conferences and seminars can be discovered via your Professional Learning Network (PLN), professional organizations, and school affiliations. Educators have the opportunity to attend and/or present at these organizations. To present, proposals are due about six months prior to the conference. Proposals are met with a selection process, and applicants are notified if their proposal was accepted or not about one to three months prior to the conference.

ACTION 14F Professional Grants

Professional organizations as well as local, state, and national professional and civic organizations offer grant funds to educators whose ideas meet the standards set by the organization. An Internet search of local funding sources will result in multiple grant opportunities. Generally, grant applications are due about six months to one year prior to acceptance.

ACTION 14G Building School Support

Developing trust, promoting a caring community that welcomes and respects differences, fostering cooperation and companionship, and otherwise creating a humane climate—these are all goals that most schools support. Furthermore, the majority of schools engage in ongoing self-evaluation to see how well the school is meeting these goals. These initial meetings provide opportunities for educators and school administrators to:

- Get to know each other.
- Explore shared interests and goals.
- Establish shared priorities for the school.
- Focus efforts on SEL.

Also, administrators work with teachers to integrate SEL principles and strategies. Setting high expectations for students, staff, and families is a means of expressing care. Many school districts throughout the world have articulated SEL as a priority in response to threats in their communities.[6] A recent publication of the International Academy of Education (IAE)—an organization that offers "timely syntheses of research-based evidence of international importance"—features the statement:

> Indeed, schools worldwide must give children intellectual and practical tools they can bring to their classrooms, families and communities. Social-emotional learning provides many of these tools. It is a way of teaching and organizing classrooms and schools that help children learn a set of skills needed to manage life tasks successfully, such as learning, forming relationships, communicating effectively, being sensitive to others' needs and getting along with others.[7]

As an engaged educator, your efforts may include bringing organizations such as the IAE to the attention of educational decision-makers and the general public in your community. Educated citizens' votes and actions can make a real difference in the lives of children.

Similarly, fostering service learning initiatives at your school will help students to foster SEL skills and knowledge by helping others in creative ways. Service learning empowers students to utilize academic skills to learn about situations of need and then to respond to those needs with collaborative efforts to serve others in the school, home, or community.

Notes

1 Seitel, 2009, p. 1.
2 Mead, cited in Seitel, 2009.
3 Merrell & Gueldner, 2010, pp. 104–105.
4 Tsabary, 2010, p. 181.
5 Mead, cited in Seitel, 2009.
6 CASEL, 2015.
7 Elias, 2015.

15

Multiple Means of Measuring Your Students' SEL[1]

For the immediate future, the evaluation of social/emotion instruction is going to be based on a combination of measures. The most prominent index will be an increase in academic learning (AL), as presented and scored by computers. This is because AL is still the preeminent goal of most schools, universally. That is changing, however.[2]

The table below presents strategies that already exist. It is likely that in the near future, electronic devices for both teaching and testing SEL will be available to all students, regardless of the economic state of the school system. This will further enhance SEL in the schools. Let us examine this list in terms of its established characteristics, as well as the authors' endorsement (or lack of it) as to the acceptable utility of each type.

One of these measurement methods is of particular interest: the open-answer technique (#7 in the table) and in particular, the "two-string" test: (#7.1 in the table).[6] This approach meets the criteria of allowing open-ended typed answers to be identified as correct or incorrect. Here is how that happens, using the "two-string" test of creative problem solving as an exemplar:

Materials Needed: a wide empty room or space; two medium-weight strings; length of each = one foot shorter than the distance from floor to ceiling (12 feet in height at most). The two strings are attached firmly to the ceiling, 14 feet apart. The simple goal is to tie the two strings together. As you can see in the drawing below, even the tallest person, holding one string, can only move about eight feet toward the other string, and thus cannot reach it. As a possible aid: a mouse trap.

Type of Measurement	Instrument name	URL	Age range	Cost	Human Scoring	Computer Scoring
1 Direct observation of student behaviors		http://hepg.org/her-home/issues/harvard-educational-review-volume-74-issue-3	3–18	H[3]	Not endorsed[4]	Not endorsed
2 Behavior rating scales	DESSA	Kaplanco.com or studentstrengths.org	6–15	M	Teachers, parents endorsed	Machine scorable, endorsed
	SEARS	http://pages.uoregon.edu/strngkds/SEARS/FelverGant2009.pdf	3–18	H	Not endorsed	Not endorsed
	Devereux Early Childhood Assessment for Preschoolers	centerforresilientchildren.org/home/dcrc-resources/	3–5	H	Not endorsed	Not endorsed
3 Self-report instruments	BERS	Proedinc.com	3–18	M	Not endorsed	Machine scorable, endorsed
	DAP	Search-institute.org	6–18	M	Not endorsed	Machine scorable, endorsed
	EQI-YV	mhs.com	5–13	M		Machine scorable, endorsed
	SEI-YV	6seconds.org/tools/sei/	7–18	M		Machine scorable, endorsed
	Youth Emotional Intelligence SEI Brain Profiles	6seconds.org/tools/sei/	7–18	M		Machine scorable, endorsed
	REACH Survey	search-institute.org/surveys/REACH?gclid=CMyJ9pPx-NACFcKPswodIcYLIg	13–18	H		Not endorsed
4 Correct answer techniques	Remote Associates test, A and B	Seymour Mednick; remote-associates-test.com/	6–13, B = 14-18	M	Not endorsed	Machine scorable, endorsed
5 Projective/ expressive techniques	Draw-a-family, ink blot	creativecounseling101.com/kinetic-family-drawing-test-art-therapy.html	3–18	H	Not endorsed	Not endorsed
		theinkblot.com/	3–18	H	Not endorsed	Not endorsed
6 Interview techniques	Ask students probing questions of their knowledge of SEL		3–18	H	Not endorsed	Not endorsed
7 Open-answer technique or essay evaluation	1. "Two-string test"	books.google.com/books?id=cpc7CJH1-s8C&pg=PA762&lpg=PA762&dq=Two-string+test+of+creativity&source (A. Maslow)	6–18	M	Not endorsed	Machine scorable, endorsed
	2. Fill in X's	markrunco.com	3–18	M	Not endorsed	Machine scorable, endorsed

Figure 15.1 Types of In-School SEL Measurement

#	Name	Description	Link/Reference	Age	L/M	Count rating	Example count
8	Fluency of examples, e.g., # of instances of self-control	Describe times when student has employed SEL		3–18	L	Count rating	Example count
9	Instances of criminal behavior, e.g., weapons found			3–18	L	Count # in folders, with severity rating	Count # in summary report, with severity rating
10	Antisocial behavior counts, e.g., verbal fights	Or brandishing a weapon on school property			L	Teacher judgment	School reports by classroom
11	Analyses of drawings: counting & pattern recognition	See Haney, W., Russell, M., & Bebell, D. (Fall 2004)		3–18	L	Not endorsed	Machine matching to templates; new but endorse
12	School attendance records by classroom				L	Not relevant	Tallies of change in daily school attendance, afterschool clubs and sports participation, pep rallies, etc.
13	Teacher behavior			3–18	L	Documentation of use of SEL materials in classroom	Not relevant
14	Shadow benefits	See Belfield, et al., 2015	Columbia's Center for Benefit-Cost Studies	3–18	M	Reduction in societal costs directly resulting from SEL	Reduction in societal costs directly resulting from SEL
15	School satisfaction survey		http://education.stateuniversity.com/pages/2392/School-Climate.html		M	Not endorsed	School, classroom specific
16	Qualitative formative assessment		http://www.edutopia.org/blog/building-sel-skills-formative-assessment-robert-marzano	3–18	M	Not endorsed at this time	Not endorsed at this time
17	Academic Learning (AL) objective scores[5]	e.g., Great Teachers and Leaders	gtlcenter.org/technical-assistance/professional-learning-modules/scoring-student-learning-objectives	6–18	L	Endorse	Endorse

Figure 15.1 (Continued)

Figure 15.2 Two-string Test

Start by attaching the two strings to the ceiling of a room, as in the drawing above. With a 10-foot-high ceiling, each string would be nine feet long. They are 14 feet apart, and there must be room for them to swing.

Tell the student: Your goal is simply to tie the two strings together. One item is available for your use in finding the solution—a mouse trap. Standing between the two strings, you should try to figure out how to tie them together, with or without the mouse trap. No matter how tall you are, you will not be able to reach the two strings, even if you try using the mouse trap to extend your reach. Do you think you can do it?

[Note: The solution appears on the next page.][7]

Many people are unable to reach this solution because they do not imagine mousetraps being used for something other than for catching mice. Here's an example of what we mean: A graduate student in psychology studied the problem and said, "I've got it! The answer is the mousetrap. You catch a bunch of mice until you get one that isn't seriously hurt. You make a pet of it, then train it to be a 'trapeze' mouse. It will jump up on one of the strings and pump back and forth until it is able to swing it over to you while you are holding the other string!" This is a good example of *functional fixity*: this student believed that a mousetrap's only function is to capture mice. His solution could conceivably work, but it is much more complicated than simply using the trap as a weight.

Most significantly, in over 3,000 administrations of the two-string test,[8] every right answer contained the word "swing," and none of the wrong answers did. In a solvable social or emotional test (has a right answer), any word which is always found in that right answer could be computer-scored. This is true whether that word is seemingly relevant to the answer or not. As long as a computer model is able to pick out the important terms, it can classify high SEL answers and distinguish them from those that are low in this capacity.

For example, suppose you wanted to reliably discriminate between student athletes who have learned social and emotional skills well, and those who have not. You might want to know this information in order to recognize which coaches are doing a good job of promoting SEL. If you could find a word or phrase that almost always appears in answers you consider correct, and almost never in wrong answers, that word or phrase would do an acceptable job of differentiating between the two.

In fact, you wouldn't even need to make a judgment of the students' answers. You might ask the regular teachers of a group of athletes to rank them on SEL. Then, if those who ranked high regularly use particular terms in each of their answers, and those ranked low don't, you have a set of questions that can be computer-scored. Get enough of such questions and you have a valid instrument.

As you can see in this chapter, SEL evaluation has come a long way in recent years. Now if we can only get education-controlling leaders to recognize the value of SEL itself . . .

Notes

1 Adapted from a submission by Dacey to *Harvard Educational Review*, *J. Neuroeducation*.
2 We dare to hope this book will contribute to that change!
3 H = High, M = Moderate, L = Low or zero cost.
4 "Not endorsed": the authors' conclusion, mostly due to high cost or unreliability of scoring.
5 Best method so long as AL predominates in the schools.
6 Krueger, 2016.
7 The mousetrap must be used to solve the problem. Attach it to one of the strings, then *SWING* it away from you. Go grasp the other string, and when the first string swings back to you, catch it. The two strings may be tied together easily.
8 Dacey and Conklin, 2013.

16

The Future of SEL

> How interesting was it to learn that the highest-paying jobs in the future will be "stempathy" jobs—jobs that combine strong science and technology skills with the ability to empathize with another human being.
>
> —Thomas Friedman

> In the future, if you want a job, you must be as unlike a machine as possible: creative, critical and socially skilled. So why are children being taught to behave like machines? Children learn best when teaching aligns with their natural exuberance, energy and curiosity. So why are they dragooned into rows and made to sit still while they are stuffed with facts?
>
> —George Monbiot

So, the future of SEL. How can this book's authors foretell its future? As you will see, most of the predictions offered in this chapter are based on new, research-based facts.[1] The rest result from educated hopefulness on our part. What is clear is that the beginnings of a tidal wave of support for SEL can be discerned in scholarly journals, professional blogs, newspaper articles, on the agenda of parent-teacher organizations, and in conversations along the sidelines at school sports events.[2] But for the present, there are some serious impediments, too.

For instance, in *5 Charts that Explain the Future of Education*,[3] Adam Shirley offers this one:

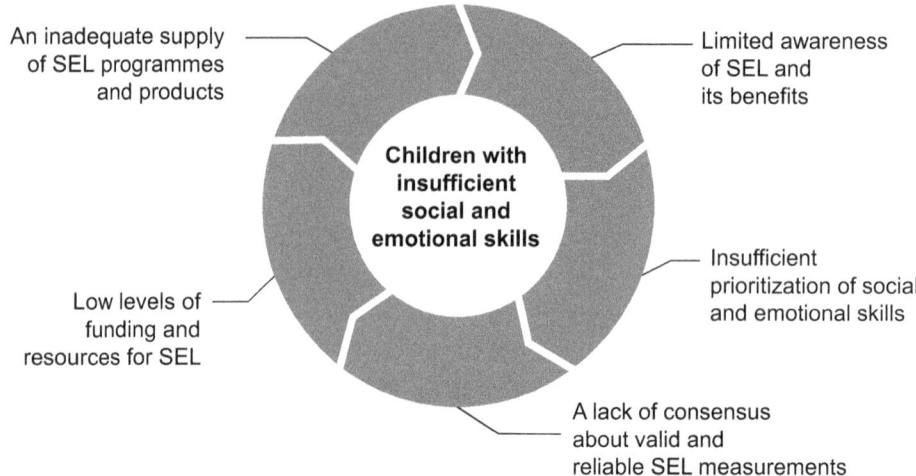

Figure 16.1 A Vicious Circle of Barriers Impedes the Adoption of SEL and Ed-Tech for SEL

Of course, Shirley is talking about SEL as independent of AL. SEL *blended* with AL will soon be seen as much more important because:

- SEL will be recognized as more responsible for success in life than AL.
- When students experience a deficit in SEL, whether due to lack of opportunity to learn or because of psychopathology, they will inevitably suffer a deficit in AL. Educational leaders will insist on a more reasonable balance between the two.
- Most teachers know that they became professional educators more because they care about SEL than because they care about AL. Increasingly, they will begin to act on their distaste for "teaching to the test" and drilling children on facts.
- The majority of parents will come to understand that scores on the SAT tests correlate only with socioeconomic level. Such scores have little relation either to success in college or success in life.
- As a result, college admissions officers will de-emphasize quantitative measures such as SATs and school grades, and will find ways to assess potential students' social and emotional skills, which do predict superior performance in college and in life.
- The power of SEL will be supported not only from the standpoint of psychology, sociology, and educational theory. It will also be proclaimed from the physical viewpoint: benefits to the human hormonal and central nervous systems.

- The analysis and improvement of school social climate have become popular topics for study. The atmosphere in classrooms will continue to receive attention, which will in turn benefit SEL.
- The continued growth of family and school alliances will foster the success of SEL.
- SEL will find its way into college classrooms, especially those in the helping professions such as psychology and sociology, as well as in STEAM-related courses (as noted in Friedman's quote at the beginning of this chapter).
- It will also begin to move into the curricula of graduate programs, most especially psychotherapy, medicine, business, and education.[4]

Facilitation of SEL Goals

- Because, understandably, "if it's not tested, it's not taught," teacher assessment will devote a much more significant role to the evaluation and educator's ability to foster SEL (see Chapter 15).
- The measurement of SEL will be based on a combination of tests presented and scored by humans and by computers. This will happen because in the foreseeable future, computers will continue to outperform humans in speed and memory, but humans will continue to outperform computers in pattern recognition, such as grasping handwriting and turning it into data. Groups of scholars are working on this aspect right now.

Breathing to Tranquility
In a Spanish Harlem second grade class, I watched a session of "breathing buddies," part of the daily routine. One by one, each child took a small stuffed animal from a cubby, found a place to sit down, and put the animal on his or her belly. Then the children watched the animals go up on an in-breath, counting 1-2-3-4-5, and down on their out-breath, to the same count. This exercise, the teacher said, leaves them calm and focused for the rest of the day. This state is hard to imagine, given the tumultuous home lives the teacher ascribed to most of the second graders in his class.[5]

Return of the Arts

STEM (science, technology, engineering, and mathematics) is currently seen in many school systems as a unified subject matter area. In the future it will be known more broadly as "STEAM," with the A standing for the arts, such as drawing, art history, music, dance, and drama. The inclusion of arts in the STEM acronym is in recognition of the value of creativity. There will be teachers who specialize in the arts, and they will emphasize the role of SEL. In addition, the effect of studying the arts on other STEM subjects will become apparent. For example, those who do well in geometry will find they are better at painting, and vice versa.

Online SEL

Electronic devices of all kinds will become as ubiquitous as the blackboards and chalk of yesteryear. These devices will make possible the cultivation of SEL through such technologies as video clips, online idea boards, computers that read body language and facial expressions, and electronic simulations. Innovative strategies may include new virtual experience video games such as *The Sims* (seen as a female game), friendship movies such as *Hunger Games*, and religion-specific programs such as OWL[6] (*Our Whole Lives*, for teaching non-sectarian sexuality values). Most likely the major concern will be the repercussions of too much use of electronics: "ECAT: everyone connected, all the time."[7]

Non-Classroom Settings for SEL

Much imaginative instruction will begin to take place outside of classrooms but within schools. For example, afterschool, weekend, and summertime programs will be held on school property.[8] Some of this education will occur in school yard settings, such as Project Adventure's ropes courses, creativity projects, moral judgment exercises, socio-drama, and socially inspirational programs. Another innovation will be awards for actions that demonstrate social and emotional excellence. Students will be instructed that when they see extraordinarily humane behavior, they should report it to school authorities, who will reward it.

Non-School Settings for SEL

Some SEL will take place in settings other than school properties altogether. For example, infant assessments for social and emotional abilities will take place in clinics, so that young children who suffer deficits can receive remedial care. Formal mediation of actual student-student and teacher-student disputes may be held in a mediator's office.

More Caring Citizens

As we have noted elsewhere in this book, there is evidence of a decline in the average person's caring for his fellow citizens. In particular, we have seen a worldwide waning of student interest in civic responsibility. As the numbers of human beings have burgeoned, especially in the biggest of our cities, our caring for each other has dropped, perhaps as a defense mechanism.

It is tremendously important that this be rectified. We believe this will be one of the top priorities of future SEL. As Daniel Goleman puts it, "Recent studies suggest that the mammalian brain circuitry for caring, on which empathic concern depends, can be strengthened with the right training and that this, in fact, makes children kinder and more generous to others."[9]

Realism

> Now [in technology] we have low cost, small size and more bandwidth. But most importantly we have social systems. Like Facebook. And that's why VR [virtual reality], AR [augmented reality] and mixed reality will not only stay, but will change everything.
>
> —Robert Scoble

In the second chapter of this book, we explored the concept of authenticity. This trait will also characterize new aspects of SEL, especially of the digital variety. As Dr. Goleman puts it, teachers should "put their learners in the driving seat and then build decision points in a learning experience based on relevant situations and choices with the same instant feedback as you would receive in a game."[10] The current term for this is "gamification." One crucial attribute of most video games is increased user retention: Just ask an 11-year-old about his favorite game, then be prepared to listen for a while! "When users remember the learned material, apply it to their real lives, and come back to learn more, you know your [gamification] project has been successful."[11]

Many games now rely on the newest electronic teachers: augmented and virtual reality. The difference between the two lies mainly in the gear. In the case of AR, the learner has an enhanced view of the material, making it more authentic. An example would be 3D movies such as *Hugo* and *Avatar*. Both films would be excellent as SEL curricula, by the way. However, that user does not control what happens on his screen.

The most stunning aspect of the future of SEL will surely be VR:

> But listen—a movie that gives one sight and sound. Suppose now I add taste, smell, even touch—is your interest taken by the story? Suppose I make it so that you are in the story, you speak to the shadows, and the shadows reply, and instead of being on a screen, the story is all about you, and you are in it.
> —Stanley Weinbaum, *Pygmalion's Spectacles*, 1935

Technologists are still working on smell and taste, but Weinbaum's "magic spectacles" eerily foreshadow the current prominence for 360-degree games, videos, and virtual worlds. Google *Expeditions* is a fine exemplar. This app allows teachers and students to take "immersive virtual journeys," such as traveling to historical landmarks, diving underwater with sharks, and visiting outer space. It requires only a cell phone and a $9 cardboard viewer! Google plans to train teachers to use VR to enhance literacy (see edu.google.com/expeditions/#about). Fields outside of education are using VR to train professionals. For example, doctors are able to use VR to practice operations, and experience what it is like to live with a mental illness such as schizophrenia.

The Ultimate Innovation: Computer to Brain and Vice Versa

> Everything about our world is going to change. And this means deep cultural change. The kind of change we saw in the 1960's when the electric guitar brought us rock'n'roll, when the pill brought us the sexual revolution, and when the space race brought us to the Moon and gave us the internet.
> —Anders Emil Møller

This next quote may *seem* fanciful, but we will not be surprised to see it happen:

> This week,[12] we got our first look at Neuralink, a new company cofounded by [Elon] Musk with a goal of building computers into our brains by way of "neural lace," a very early-stage technology that lays

on your brain and bridges it to a computer. It's the next step beyond even that blending of the digital and physical worlds, as human and machine become one.

Assuming the science works—and lots of smart people believe that it will—this is the logical endpoint of the road that smartphones started us on. If smartphones gave us access to information and augmented reality puts that information in front of us when we need it, then putting neural lace in our brains just closes the gap. Musk has said this is because the rise of artificial intelligence—which underpins a lot of the other technologies, including voice assistants and virtual reality—means humans will have to augment themselves just to keep up with the machines. If you're curious about this idea, futurist Ray Kurzweil is the leading voice on the topic.[13]

More Research

There is one more area that we think will benefit SEL greatly: government and privately-funded research. As we have pointed out in numerous places in this book, there is growing consensus among instructional leaders, activist parents, and indeed the general public. The whole world needs to do a better job of fostering SEL, and that will mean carefully controlled experiments and evaluations. Throughout the 20th and so far in the 21st centuries, huge amounts of money have been spent on how to promote academic learning. Although SEL has suffered from an almost complete dearth of such support, we feel confident that this is about to change.

In summary, "Teaching SEL will become equally important [as AL], as our social media gradually changes too, further breaking down the barriers of location and communication."[14] We are seeing examples in the work of, for example, the excellent 6Seconds[15] program. This change is real, and that is why we believe AL embedded with SEL is, universally, the future of education. We hope our book will assist you in making this revolution take place.

Notes

1 Dusenbury and Weissberg, April 2017.
2 CASEL, 2016; Weissberg, 2016; Zakrzewski, 2015, p. 1.
3 Shirley, 2016, p. 1.
4 Goleman, Boyatzis, and McKee, 2013.

5 N. Bryan, personal communication.
6 UUA, 2017.
7 Kurzweil, 2012, p. 21.
8 Dacey, 1980.
9 Goleman, 2015, p. 593.
10 Goleman, cited in Coppens, 2016, p. 1.
11 Hughes, 2016, p. 1.
12 Weinberger, April 2, 2017.
13 Kurzweil, 2006, 2012.
14 Lawrie, 2017, p. 1.
15 6Seconds.org, 2016.

References

AFSP. (2016). *Risk factors and warning signs*. Retrieved from afsp.org/about-suicide/risk-factors-and-warning-signs/

American Academy of Child and Adolescent Psychiatry. (2011). *Number 80*. Retrieved from aacap.org/AACAP/Families_and_Youth/Facts_for_Families/Facts_for_Families_Pages/Bullying_80.aspx

Armed Forces & Society: An Interdisciplinary Journal. (2004). *Bibliography 34*(4), 382.

ASCD. (2016, November). *Webinar on implementing SEL*. Retrieved from www.ascd.org/public-policy/EducatorAdvocates.aspx?EventID=3557902711&FirstName=John&LastName=Dacey&Email=dacey%40bc.edu&EnrollmentID=

Baird, I. (2014). *A mindful cure to bullying*. Retrieved from www.huffingtonpost.com/izzy-baird/bullying_b_5591930.html

Belfield, C., et al. (2015). The economic value of social and emotional learning. Center for Benefit-Cost Studies in Education, Teachers College, Columbia University. http://www.cbcse.org

Bergland, C. (2016). *10 ways mindfulness and meditation promote well-being*. Retrieved from psychologytoday.com/blog/the-athletes-way/201504/10-ways-mindfulness-and-meditation-promote-well-being

Bethell, C.D., Newacheck, P., Hawes, E., & Halfon, N. (2014). Adverse childhood experiences: Assessing the impact on health and school engagement and the mitigating role of resilience. *Health Affairs*. December 2014, *33*(12), 2106–2115, doi:10.1377/hlthaff.2014.0914

Blad, E. (2015). Survey: Student success calls for more than academic skills: Social-emotional skills matter. *EdWeek*. Retrieved from edweek.org

Breedlove, C. (2017). Spiritual muscle, courage, and non-compliance. *Cbreedlove@Uua.Org*, p. 2.

Bridgeland, J., Bruce, M., & Hariharan, A. (2013). The missing piece: A national teacher survey on how social and emotional learning can empower children and transform schools. *Collaborative for Academic, Social, and Emotional Learning*. Retrieved from casel.org/library/the-missing-piece

Brooks, D. (2014). *The organization kid*. The Atlantic Monthly Group. Retrieved from theatlantic.com/magazine/archive/2001/04/the-organization-kid/302164/

Burton, D., & Raedeke, T. (2014). *Coaches key in making competition a positive or negative sport experience for athletes*. Retrieved from humankinetics.com/excerpts/excerpts/coaches-key-in-making-competition-a-positive-or-negative-sport-experience-for-athletes

Carrizales-Engelmann, D., et al. (2016, May). *Strong kids—grades 3–5: A social and emotional learning curriculum (Strong Kids Curricula)* (2nd ed.). New York: Brooks.

CASEL. (2016). *SEL research*. Retrieved from casel.org/research/#Field

CCSS. (2015). *Core standards*. Retrieved from ReCorestandards.org

Clarebout, G., Horz, H., Schnotz, W., & Elen, J. (2010). The relations between self-regulation and the embedding of support in learning environments. *Educational Technology Research and Development, 58*(5), 573–587.

Cohen, J. (Ed). (2011). *Caring classrooms, intelligent schools: The social emotional education of young children*. New York: Teachers College Press.

Cohn, B. (2017). *Question your answers*, p. 1. Retrieved from mail.google.com/mail/u/0/#inbox/15a432a9178a3099

Coleman. J. (1969). *The adolescent society*. Glencoe, Illinois: The Free Press.

Cressey, J., Bettencourt, J., Donahue-Keegan, D., Villegas-Reimers, E., & Wong, C. (2017). *Social-emotional learning in teacher education: A needs assessment survey of teacher educators*. Boston, MA: Massachusetts Consortium for Social-Emotional Learning in Teacher Education.

Dacey, J. (Ed.). (1980). *Where the world is*. Glenview, IL: Goodyear.

Dacey, J. (1989a). *Fundamentals of creative thinking*. Lexington, MA: D. C. Heath/Lexington Books.

Dacey, J. (1989b). Peak periods of creative growth across the life span. *Journal of Creative Behavior, 23*(4), 224–247.

Dacey, J. (1989c). Discriminating characteristics of the families of highly creative adolescents. *Journal of Creative Behavior, 23*(4), 263–271.

Dacey, J. (2011a). A history of the concept of creativity. In H. Gardner & R. Sternberg (Eds.), *Encyclopedia of creativity* (3 Vols., 2nd ed.). San Francisco, CA: Academic Press.

Dacey, J. (2011b). Child safety: Doing the most you can to keep your kids safe. *Parent Guide News*. Retrieved from parentguidenews.com/Catalog/Toddler/ChildSafety

Dacey, J. (2015). History of creativity. In *Encyclopedia of creativity* (3 Vols., 2nd ed.). San Francisco, CA: Academic Press.

Dacey, J., Amara, D., & Seavey, G. (1993, Winter). Reducing dropout rate in inner city middle school children through instruction in self control. *Research on Middle Level Education, 202*, 91–103.

Dacey, J., & Conklin, W. (2013). *Creativity and the standards*. Huntington Beach, CA: TCM/Shell.

Dacey, J., deSalvatore, L., & Robinson, J. (1997). The results of teaching middle school students two relaxation techniques as part of a conflict prevention program. *Research on Middle Level Education, 20*(2), 91–102.

Dacey, J., & Fiore, L. (2000). *Your anxious child*. San Francisco, CA: Jossey-Bass/Wiley.

Dacey, J., & Fiore, L. (2006). *The safe child handbook: How to protect your family and cope with anxiety in a threat-filled world*. New York: Wiley.

Dacey, J., Fiore, L., & Brion-Meisels, S. (2016a). *Your anxious child*. Chichester, England: Houghton/Mifflin-Wiley-Blackstone.

Dacey, J., Fiore, L., & Brion-Meisels, S. (2016b). *Your child's social and emotional well-being*. Chichester, England: Houghton-Mifflin/Wiley.

Dacey, J., Kenny, M., & Margolis, D. (2008). *Adolescent development* (3rd ed.). New York: Thompson.

Dacey, J., & Lennon, K. (1999). *Understanding creativity: The interplay of biological, psychological and social factors*. San Francisco, CA: Jossey-Bass.

Dacey, J., & Packer, A. (1992). *The nurturing parent*. New York: Simon & Schuster.

Dacey, J. & Ripple, R. (1969). Relationships of some adolescent characteristics and verbal creativity. *Psychology in the Schools, 6*(3): 321–324.

Dacey, J., Travers, J., & Fiore, L (2009). *Human development across the lifespan* (7th ed.). New York and Boston, MA: McGraw-Hill.

Dacey, J., & Weygint, L. (2002). *The joyful family*. San Francisco, CA: Conari.

Das, K. (2013). *The quantum guide to life: How the laws of physics explain our lives from laziness to love*. New York: Skyhorse.

Datta, N. (2016). *Positive thinking: How to foster in your child*. Retrieved from aboutkids health.ca/En/HealthAZ/FamilyandPeerRelations/life-skills/Pages/Positive-thinking-How-to-foster-in-your-child.aspx

deBono, E. (1993). *Teach your child how to think*. New York: Viking.

De Bruin, A.B., Thiede, K.W., & Camp, G. (2011). Generating keywords improves metacomprehension and self-regulation in elementary and middle school children. *Journal of Experimental Child Psychology, 109*(3), 294–310.

Dunning-Kruger effect. (2014). Wikipedia.com

Dusenbury, L., & Weissberg, R. (2017, April). *Social emotional learning in elementary school: Preparation for success*. University Park, PA: Robert Wood Johnson Foundation/Penn State.

Elias, M.J. (2003). *Academic and social-emotional learning*. Brussels, Belgium: International Academy of Education.

Elstad, E., & Turmo, A. (2010). Students' self-regulation and teacher's influence in science: Interplay between ethnicity and gender. *Research in Science & Technological Education, 28*(3), 249–260.

Erikson, E.H. (1950). *Childhood and society*. New York: Norton & Co.

Fantz, A. (2015). *Prison time for some Atlanta school educators in cheating scandal*. Retrieved from CNN.com

Flannick, J., et al. (2014). Loss-of-function mutations in SLC30A8 protect against type 2 diabetes. Nature Genetics, 46(4): 357–363.

Galinsky, E. (2010). *Mind in the making: The seven essential life skills every child needs*. NAEYC (special ed.). New York: HarperCollins.

Gilbert, I. (2014). *Independent thinking*. Carmarthen, UK: Independent Thinking Press.

Gladwell, M. (2005). *Blink: The power of thinking without thinking*. New York: Back Bay Books.

Goleman, D. (2014). The triple focus: A new approach to education, with Peter Senge. *More Than Sound.*

Goleman, D. (2015). *A force for good: The Dalai Lama's vision for our world.* New York: Bantam Books.

Goleman, D. Cited in Coppens, A. (2016). *What are the most effective uses of gamification in learning?* Retrieved from elearningindustry.com/free-ebooks/gamification-reshapes-learning

Goleman, D., Boyatzis, R., & McKee. A. (2013). *Primal leadership: unleashing the power of emotional intelligence.* Cambridge, MA: Harvard Press.

Greenfield, K. (2011). *The myth of choice: Personal responsibility in a world of limits.* New Haven: Yale University Press.

Haney, W., Russell, M., & Bebell, D. (Fall 2004). Drawing on education: Using drawings to document schooling and support change. *Harvard Educational Review,* 74(3), 241–272.

Henning, G., Tha, M., & Meers, T. (2014). *Epidemiology.* New York: Springer.

Henry's Freedom Box. (2016). Retrieved from the-best-childrens-books.org

Hughes, A. (2016). *What are the most effective uses of Gamification in Learning?* Retrieved from elearningindustry.com/how-gamification-reshapes-learning#andrew-hughes

Johnson, D., Johnson, R., & Stamme, B. (2000). *Cooperative learning methods: A meta-analysis.* Minneapolis, MN: University of Minnesota Press.

Kabat-Zinn, J. (2013). *Full catastrophe living (revised edition): Using the wisdom of your body and mind to face stress, pain, and illness.* New York: Bantam.

Kim, K.H. (2010). The creativity crisis in the United States. *Online Encyclopedia Brittanica,* p 2.

Kolovelonis, A., Goudas, M., & Dermitzaki, I. (2011). The effect of different goals and self-recording on self-regulation of learning a motor skill in a physical education setting. *Learning and Instruction,* 21(3), 355–364.

Krueger, J. (2016). *Maslow on creativity.* Retrieved from psychologytoday.com/blog/one-among-many/201309/maslow-creativity

Kurzweil, R. (2006). *The singularity is near.* New York: Viking.

Kurzweil, R. (2012). *How to create a mind: The secret of human thought revealed.* New York: Viking.

Labuhn, A.S., Zimmerman, B.J., & Hasselhorn, M. (2010). Enhancing students' self-regulation and mathematics performance: The influence of feedback and self-evaluative standards. *Metacognition and Learning,* 5(2), 173–194.

Lawrie, G. (2017). *How our school is using Virtual Reality to prepare pupils for a future dominated by technology.* Retrieved from telegraph.co.uk/education/2017/01/23/school-using-virtual-reality-prepare-pupils-future-dominated/

Marcoz. H. (2015). *How well do you know yourself?* helenemarcoz.net

Maclean, A. (2008). *The privileges of rank: The peacetime draft and later-life attainment.* Bethesda, MD: National Center for Biotechnology Information.

Maslow, A.H. (1998). *Books, Articles.* www.maslow.com

Maslow, A.H. (1998). *Toward a psychology of being, 3/e*. New York: John Wiley & Sons, Inc.

Masten, A.S. (2014). Global perspectives on resilience in children and youth. *Child Development, 85*(1): 6–20. doi:10.1111/cdev.12205

McCloud, C., & Martin, K. (2008). *Fill a bucket: a guide to daily happiness*. Northville, MI: Nelson Publishing.

Mead, M. Cited in Seitel, M. (2009). Mindfulness in a school community. In I. McHenry & R. Brady (Eds.), *Tuning in: Mindfulness in teaching & learning*. Philadelphia, PA: Friends Council on Education.

Merrell, K., & Carrizales-Engelmann, D. (2007). *Strong kids—grades 3–5: A social and emotional learning curriculum (strong kids curricula)*. New York: Paul H. Brookes Publishing Co.

Merrell, K. & Gueldner, B. (2010). *Social and emotional learning in the classroom: Promoting mental health and academic success*. New York: Guilford Press.

MomsFightBack.org (2017). *Bullying*. Retrieved from http://momsfightback.org/topics/bullying/

Nadworny, E. (2016, November). *Middle school suicides reach an all-time high*. Retrieved from npr.org/sections/ed/2016/11/04/500659746/middle-school-suicides-reach-an-all-time-high

National Center for School Engagement. (2016). *Rachel's challenge*. Retrieved from rachelschallenge.org/about-us?gclid=CNL1hqKz9NACFcSPswodE8wBIA

NCTM. (2016a). *Beginning to problem solve with "I notice, I wonder."* Retrieved from http://mathforum.org/pubs/notice_wonder_intro.pdf

NCTM. (2016b). *I notice, I wonder*. Retrieved from mathforum.org/pubs/notice_wonder_intro.pdf

Paulos, J. (2016, July). *Do sat scores really predict success?* Retrieved from http://abcnews.go.com/technology/whoscounting/story?id=98373&page=1

Payton, J., Weissburg, R., Durlak, J., Dymnicki, A., Taylor, R., Schellinger, K., & Pachan, M. (2015). *The positive impact of social and emotional learning for kindergarten to eighth-grade student: Findings from three scientific reviews*. Retrieved from CASEL.org.

Petersen, K. (2012). *Activities for building character and social-emotional learning grades 3–5 (Safe & Caring Schools®)*. Minneapolis, MN: Free Spirit Publishing Inc.

Prakash, B. (2012, March 2). *Emotional intelligence for an empathetic society. Six seconds EQ network*. Retrieved from 6seconds.org/

Richhtart, R., Church, M., & Morrison, K. (2011). *Making thinking visible*. San Francisco, CA: Jossey/Bass.

Rifkin, J. (2009). *The empathic civilization*. New York: Penguin.

Scelfo, J. (2015, November). *Teaching peace in Elementary School*. Retrieved from nytimes.com/2015/11/15/sunday-review/teaching-peace-in-elementary-school.html?smid=nytcore-iphone-share&smprod=nytcore-iphone

Schank, R., & Cleary, C. (1995). *Making machines creative*. Cambridge, MA: MIT University Press.

Schunk, D., & Zimmerman, B. (2007). Influencing children's self-efficacy and self-regulation of reading and writing through modeling. *Reading & Writing Quarterly*, 23(1), 7–25.

Seitel, M. (2009). Mindfulness in a school community. In I. McHenry & R. Brady (Eds.), *Tuning in: Mindfulness in teaching & learning*. Philadelphia, PA: Friends Council on Education.

Selman, R. (2003). *The promotion of social awareness*. New York: Russell Sage Foundation.

Selye, H. (1956). *The stress of life*. New York: McGraw-Hill.

Scriven, M., & Paul, R. (1987). Critical thinking definitions. Paper read at the *8th Annual International Conference on Critical Thinking and Education Reform*.

Shapiro, D., et al. (1993). A psychological "sense-of-control" profile of patients with anorexia nervosa and bulimia nervosa. *Psychological Reports*: 73, 531–541.

Shirley, A. (2016). *Five charts that explain the future of education*, p. 1. Retrieved from weforum.org/agenda/2016/05/5-charts-that-explain-the-future-of-education/

Shriver, T., & Buffett, J. (2015). The uncommon core. In J. Durlak, C. Domitrovich, R. Weissburg, & T. Gullotta (Eds.), *Handbook of social and emotional learning: Research and practice* (pp. xv–xvi). New York: Guilford.

Six Seconds. (2016). *Six seconds EQ network*. Retrieved from 6seconds.org/

Slavin, R. (2013). Why use cooperative learning? *Starting Point: Teaching Entry Level Geoscience*. Retrieved from https://serc.carleton.edu/introgeo/cooperative/whyuse.html

Sternberg, R., & Lubart, T. (1995). *Defying the crowd*. New York: Free Press.

Stevens, T. (2015). The case for being a generous leader: Are you a generous leader or a selfish one? http://www.fastcompany.com/3043572/

Torrance, E. (2000). *Voyages of discovering creativity*. New York: Praeger.

Transforming Education (2017). *Experts are saying*. Retrieved from CASEL.org

Tsabary, S. (2010). *The conscious parent: Transforming ourselves, empowering our children*. Vancouver, Canada: Namaste Publishing.

U.U.A. (2017). *Our whole lives: Lifespan sexuality education*. Retrieved from https://www.uua.org/re/owl

van Noorden, T., Bukowski, W.M., Haselager, G.J.T., Lansu, T.A.M. and Cillessen, A.H.N. (2016). Disentangling the frequency and severity of bullying and victimization in the association with empathy. *Social Development*, 25(1): 176–192, doi:10.1111/sode.12133

Weinberger, M. (2017, April 2). The smartphone is eventually going to die, and then things are going to get really crazy. *Business Insider*. Retrieved from businessinsider.in/the-smartphone-is-eventually-going-to-die-and-then-things-are-going-to-get-really-crazy/articleshow/57977438.cms

Weissberg, R. (2016a). *Consensus statement to the U.S. D.O.E.* Chicago: Collaborative for Academic, Social and Emotional Learning.

Weissberg, R. (2016b). *Why social and emotional learning is essential for students*. Retrieved from edutopia.org/blog/why

Weng, H. Y., Fox, A. S., Shackman, A. J., Stodola, D. E., Caldwell, J. Z. K., Olson, M. C., Rogers, G. M., & Davidson, R. J. (2013). Compassion training alters altruism and the neural responses to suffering. *Psychological Science, 24*, 1171–1180.

Zakrzewski, F. (2015). *Social-emotional learning: Why now?* Retrieved from huffingtonpost.com/vicki-zakrzewski-phd/social-emotional-learning-why-now_b_6466918.html

Zernike, K. (2015, October 24). Obama administration calls for limits on testing in schools. *New York Times.*

Zhao, Y. (2014). *Who's afraid of the big bad dragon: Why china has the best (and worst) education system in the world*. San Francisco, CA: Jossey-Bass.

Zimmerman, B. J. (2000). Attaining self-regulation: a social cognitive perspective. In M. Boekaerts, P. R. Pintrich, & M. Zeidner, (Eds.), *Handbook of Self-Regulation*. San Diego, CA: Academic Press.